THE FASCINATION OF
WHAT'S DIFFICULT

THE FASCINATION OF WHAT'S DIFFICULT

A Life of Maud Gonne

Kim Bendheim

OR Books

New York · London

All rights information: rights@orbooks.com
Visit our website at www.orbooks.com

First printing 2021

Published by OR Books, New York and London

© 2021 Kim Bendheim

Library of Congress Cataloging-in-Publication Data: A catalog record for this book is available from the Library of Congress.

Typeset by Lapiz Digital Services. Printed by Bookmobile, USA, and CPI, UK.

paperback ISBN 978-1-68219-206-1 • ebook ISBN 978-1-68219-209-2

Contents

The fascination of what's difficult
Has dried the sap out of my veins, and rent
Spontaneous joy and natural content
Out of my heart. There's something ails our colt
That must, as if it had not holy blood
Nor on Olympus leaped from cloud to cloud,
Shiver under the lash, strain, sweat and jolt
As though it dragged road metal. My curse on plays
That have to be set up in fifty ways,
On the day's war with every knave and dolt,
Theatre business, management of men.
I swear before the dawn comes round again
I'll find the stable and pull out the bolt.

> — William Butler Yeats,
>   "The Fascination of What's Difficult"

Is there no way to make the past the present,
To wind and unwind it like a ball of yarn?

> — Murasaki Shikibu, *The Tale of Genji*

Prologue

This biography is partly the tale of how several lives entwined through the centuries: Maud Gonne's with that of the celebrated Irish poet W. B. Yeats, who wrote poetry to and about her for forty-three years, and hers with mine for the last twenty-five years. She was his muse but she was also an Irish political activist, a noted human rights speaker, a journalist at a time when women journalists were rare. Altogether she played a far greater role in western European history than she is given credit for. In Ireland, but not without, she is justly celebrated as an agent for change. Most biographies focus on her relationship with Yeats, or on the persona she presented the public rather than the amazing tale of her own life which had a lasting effect on thousands and thousands of people on both sides of the Atlantic. She was much more than a muse.

I first encountered Maud Gonne in 1993 when I reviewed the collection of Gonne-Yeats letters, edited by her granddaughter Anna MacBride White and A. Norman Jeffares, the noted Irish literary scholar. I was living in Los Angeles and writing a "Book Beat" column on new Irish literature for a LA-based Irish monthly. I'd been entranced by Irish literature since college and reviewed some wonderful Irish books for the *Los Angeles Times* that I still cherish.

Reading the letters, I became seduced not, as one might expect, by the great poet's few surviving letters to her, but by Maud's voice on the page. What the letters unravel, like a lovely colored ball of string, is the connection between Yeats and Gonne and the uniqueness of her voice. She encouraged him in his quest for Irish subjects, Irish myths and legends, and supported his celebration of the particularities of holy places and geographic landscapes in Ireland.

Her own voice is singular, irreverent, and smart. She was a formidable political agitator, a feminist before the term was coined. She was prophetic. On August 26, 1914, at the beginning of the Great War, she wrote Yeats:

> This war is an inconceivable madness which has taken hold of Europe. It is unlike any war that has ever been.... The victor will be nearly as enfeebled as the vanquished.... Could the women, who are after all the guardians of the race, end it? ...
> I always felt the wave of the woman's power was rising, the men are destroying themselves & we are looking on.

In the first month of the conflict, she predicted the scope of World War I; due to its use of modern weapons, technology, and chemicals to extinguish an estimated 40 million human lives, it would prove to be the deadliest war in history. She wrote with heart and passion about things that mattered, including the terrible conditions of Irish political prisoners in British jails.

Years later as an NYU graduate student, at the suggestion of my professor, I wrote a paper on Yeats's images of Maud as Helen of Troy. It left me wanting to know even more about her life. Who was she, apart from a love object in Yeats's poetry? Helen of Troy's beauty sparked a war—and Ulysses's ten-year odyssey home to his wife, the clever, patient Penelope—but Maud had a full life outside of Yeats's poems. My dawning feminism grew along with my curiosity about Maud Gonne. This curiosity has endured over two decades and was finally quenched by writing this book.

I was fortunate in the course of my own odyssey to meet warm, interesting people, including Maud's granddaughter Anna MacBride White, a lovely woman who with her husband, a kindly vet, welcomed me into their Dublin home. We had tea in the garden.

Then two years ago in New York, chatting at a holiday party, I told a publisher about my interest in Maud Gonne. He wanted to know if I'd thought of doing a book on her. I said yes and submitted a short proposal. We had a pleasant lunch to discuss, and he followed up by commissioning me to write a book. Maud Gonne had been at the back of my mind for decades, so I jumped at the chance. This biography, my first book, became a way of figuring out why her character had such resonance with mine and who this elusive, theatrical woman really was: a fiery patriot, a political prisoner, a mother? A clever wealthy woman who wielded her great fortune to successfully promote the cause of Irish nationalism? Or all the above?

In the hunt to penetrate the mysteries of Maud's character, and explain her enduring allure, I returned to Dublin. On this trip, besides going to the National Library of Ireland, I tracked down two of her great-granddaughters, Iseult White and Laragh Stuart, and had lunch with each of them. Wildly different, each woman was engaging in her own way. Iseult is the executor of her mother Anna MacBride White's literary estate. I met with her first, which was relatively easy to arrange as I had known her mother and sister from my first few visits to Dublin.

Before our rendezvous, I researched Iseult White. On her website, she describes herself as an experienced global market manager for technology companies in Silicon Valley where she lived and worked for a number of years. Then, after having completed a master's program in psychotherapy, she reinvented herself in Ireland as a management consultant, executive coach, and psychotherapist. At Iseult's suggestion, we arranged a brunch on a Sunday in November at the airy, elegant Layla's Terrace on the rooftop of the Devlin Hotel in Ranelagh. We were practically the only ones in the restaurant that morning, so she was easy to pick out when she walked in: a confident, middle-aged woman with gorgeous skin and green eyes. The mother of two daughters, she had a solid, grounded presence and straight, perhaps blown-out, shoulder-length red hair. At the restaurant she was very particular, ordering a soy cappuccino and porridge with the extras on the side. When it came, she said, "I asked for a piping hot soy milk cappuccino and that is not. Take it back." And they did.

Here was a woman who knew what she wanted and insisted on getting it. In our conversation, after our first flurry of hellos, she emerged as a strong feminist. Speaking of Maud's parenting, she said, "A child of that class was not raised by their mother." She elaborated: "The myth of motherhood emerged postwar as a way to keep women out of the workplace and give the men back their old jobs."

She dryly remarked of Yeats's extensive commentary on Maud, "as if he were a valid source of information on Madame!" Iseult called her great-grandmother *Madame*, as she was known in Ireland during the last thirty years of her life. Patiently, Iseult spelled out the complicated connections between myriad cousins and told me that her grandfather, Seán MacBride, didn't make any money until the 1940s or 50s, "because he obviously defended all the Republican prisoners for free." He and his family, including Maud who lived with them, survived on Maud's inheritance. Iseult was visibly proud of her grandfather, whom she knew as a child. As a small child at the time, she was of course aware he'd been awarded the 1974 Nobel Peace Prize for cofounding Amnesty International.

Iseult couldn't answer basic questions about her great-grandmother, since she hadn't known her personally, just through stories. I asked, was Maud Gonne six feet tall? How tall was the woman billed as "a goddess"? Iseult didn't know, but was helpful in other ways. After brunch, she offered to drive me to Roebuck House, where Madame spent the final decades of her life, with her daughter-in-law known as "Kid," her son Seán and their two children, Anna and Tiernan MacBride. We parted, and Iseult drove off. Then I walked around Roebuck House. It looked much as it did in pictures, a big two-story brick structure, except instead of a garden in back there was a parking lot.

In interviews on the web, Iseult discussed how "as a child creativity was my friend. Reading, writing, painting, piano, and ballet created sanctuary from a childhood punctured by trauma." Singular in the current tell-all climate, she refused in-person and via email to discuss the source of her trauma, only explaining that "it should be possible to talk about PTSD without having to describe the trauma." She further added in an email: "If I ever talk/write about the trauma it will be in my own words." Iseult is the author of *The Mindfulness Workout: A Guide to Mental Fitness for Teenagers and the Adults in Their Lives,* so perhaps one day she will indeed write a book about it.

After meeting with Iseult, I located Laragh Stuart, the granddaughter of Maud's illegitimate daughter Iseult Gonne. Laragh's great-grandfather was Lucien Millevoye, while Iseult White's was John MacBride—two very different men. Like her cousin, Laragh made a vivid impression: she's a smart, slight, ethereal woman with long wavy reddish-brown blond hair. Also a mother, she'd successfully run her own business for twenty-one years, in Dublin, selling delicious-sounding sauces and soups like beetroot, dill, and crème fraîche. On Instagram, her brand is described as "the creators of fine arts soups and sauces taken from the soil and made by humans, additive-free and gluten-free." Since we met for lunch in November 2018, she has shuttered that business and pivoted into art photography. Not surprising that she has been preoccupied with art: Laragh's father, Ian, was the well-regarded Irish sculptor Ian Stuart. In his day, he exhibited at the Paris Biennale, in galleries in Dublin, and museums in New York and London.

Laragh and I arranged via email to meet inside the entrance to the grand Shelbourne Hotel. She had just returned via Paris from a trip to Cambodia with her fourteen-year-old son. Inside, we went to the Horseshoe Bar. Laragh said that her father would take her there for lunch, a happy memory from her peripatetic childhood. When she was little, she learned to walk in the VW van that her parents bought to drive with her and her sister to India. In India, they lived on a houseboat. At twelve, she was sent to boarding school in England. "I didn't know the alphabet. I would go into the kindergarten room at night to learn to read. I was embarrassed, but at the end of the year, I was up to the level of the other children."

Laragh is now forty-eight. Like her cousin Iseult, she obviously suffered some trauma in her childhood, making me wonder at the different ways women can be resilient and overcome their pasts. Clearly Laragh still missed her father, though he was a much older father to her and her two sisters. Ian had married Laragh's mother, Anna, whom he knew because she had been a schoolfriend of one of his three daughters by his first wife, the artist Imogen Stuart. The family, as I was learning firsthand, was quite complicated, filled with half sisters and brothers and cousins. As Iseult White remarked, "In Ireland growing up it was very unusual. I never knew if people were friends of the family or cousins." Laragh had the same issue. At lunch, she speculated that "maybe Lucien Millevoye wasn't Iseult's father." In a follow-up email, she suggested, "Maybe it was Yeats."

It felt as if I were looking through a telescope down through the generations. Each of the two women, via two different men, provided a glimpse into the Maud Gonne of the past. Though neither of the two had known her, both grew up hearing plenty of stories about her, Iseult from her grandfather Seán MacBride and from her mother, the editor Anna MacBride White, who was partly raised by her grandmother Maud. Laragh would have heard stories from her father, the talkative Ian Stuart who, a generation older than Laragh's mother, had known his mother and grandmother quite well. My own perception of this complicated woman, Maud Gonne, developed and changed over the course of the two years it took to research and write her biography. I hope it will give readers yet another angle from which to view Maud Gonne, an international celebrity of her era. Though at birth Maud had been blessed with many gifts—looks, intelligence, and her own fortune—growing up she was an emotional orphan. Her mother died when she was four. Her tender, caring father, a captain in the British Army, posted all over the empire, was away for long stretches of time. He was literally unavailable. Like Princess Di, her empathy for others outside her social bubble seemed infinite. Unlike other debutantes, she found a cause greater than herself to dedicate her life to: that of Ireland, then solidly under Britain's boot and the poorest, most rural country in Western Europe. As an activist, she took on the daunting task of toppling the British Empire by any means possible, including force.

One of the reasons Maud intrigued me was that, though she lived more than one hundred fifty years ago, in some ways her life seemed strangely familiar. When it came to men, Maud's fortune complicated her romantic life. Her financial assets, while empowering her, were intimidating to men. I understood, because I too have felt money as a burden when dating.

I have insight into obsessive and tormented love like Yeats's for Maud—he proposed four times—because I was pursued by a man for years and years while I was preoccupied with my own unrequited love for a restless philanderer. The role of obsession and love for creative artists, the questions of real love versus passing fancy or fruitless obsession, of when the torment outweighs the pleasure—these continue to intrigue me as a writer and as a woman.

The last American biography of Maud Gonne was published forty years ago. It does not deal with her great wealth, concluding she had "a modest income." The very title of a 2016 Irish biography, *The Adulterous Muse*, belittles the woman. No one has ever written a biography of Yeats and called it *The Adulterous Poet*, although he too had a first affair with a married woman. Now that the debate triggered by the Me Too movement has broadened to include women's rights and basic issues of social justice all over the world, her life, loves, and contributions in these areas should be reevaluated. With the worldwide ascendance of dictators and the growing censorship of freedom of expression, the rights of protestors and of political prisoners, which Maud championed for decades, remains an international issue.

The dangers as well as the glories of transcendent nationalism is another timely topic. Currently numerous people choose to martyr themselves in order to murder civilians, giving themselves moments of fame on international TV. Maud is the happy example of a fanatic who, in the course of her long life, became an admirer of leaders who used peaceful means to achieve radical political ends.

In researching this biography these last two years, I learned that the challenges facing a woman born in 1866 remain resonant for women today. We women continue to struggle with questions of political power, money, and independence; we struggle with the question of how to find a loving partner and how to see peace, not war, reign over our planet.

When I began this project, I admired Maud as a strong woman who pursued a challenging path. She was a rousing leader for the cause of Irish nationalism after centuries of exploitation by the British. She became the inspiration for Yeats, one of the greatest poets in the English language, but she was my heroine because instead of just being a debutante, she was a rebel. She forged a highly effective political path before women had the vote or the right to keep their own property under their name when they married in France or in the United States. England had only changed its onerous laws regarding married women's property rights in 1882. An unmarried upper-class young woman would normally be accompanied in public by her parents, another relative or spinster as chaperone. Single upper-class young women did not often travel alone and if they did they became prey, like the heroine of a Henry James novel. Maud evaded that fate.

In the process of researching this biography I learned that Maud Gonne was a complex, difficult woman. As I intuited, there was a lot more going on in her life than the little I learned about her in my twentieth-century lit class at NYU. Not all aspects of her character appealed. For instance, I was horrified to discover she was a lifelong anti-Semite, especially given my growing cultural affiliation as a Jew. Nor, I discovered, was she the woman whose image she projected out into the world: that of an Irish Joan of Arc.

Maud Gonne was neither Irish by birth nor by heritage, unless you count one Irish great-grandparent. Nor, like Joan, to whom the press compared her, was she a teenager. She was the mother of two children, one out of wedlock. She lived a long life and died at home, aged eighty-seven, with her daughter-in-law, two grandchildren, and lifelong friends. The real Joan of Arc was a nineteen-year-old virgin burned alive by the English as a heretic and witch. In the nineteenth century, the Catholic Church began the long process of transforming Joan's reputation, declaring her a saint in 1920.

What did Joan and Maud Gonne, an Irish nationalist celebrated in three countries for her looks, her journalism, and her eloquent public speaking, have in common? Did Maud Gonne pull off one of the biggest publicity shams of the century? Did she accomplish much good in the world? If so, what lives on after her? I had many questions and by now my own obsession with Maud Gonne. This book is the result.

Chapter 1
An English Girl's Irish Childhood

Born in 1866, Maud Gonne was an unusual Irish rebel. She came from one of England's wealthiest families, and she was a woman. Irish women were not accepted into men's Irish nationalist societies until the turn of the next century. She was born to an English family, but had one Irish great-grandparent. She said different things at different times about her Irish forebears. Regardless, from these disparate elements, she forged a veritable shield of an identity, one that enabled her to be known as the Irish Joan of Arc.

At his death in 1869, her grandfather William Cook was one of the richest men in England, leaving a fortune of £2 million, roughly equivalent to $200 million today. His fortune was divided among his five children, one of whom was Maud's mother Edith. Maud's inheritance from her mother fueled her unpaid work for Ireland. Like her grandfather, she was clever.

William Cook started out selling linens and drapes in north London as an apprentice; he came from a sheep farm in Norfolk. Moving up in the linen business, he opened a wholesale warehouse with a partner, then continued the business under his own name. It grew and he took in his brother James as a partner. "The concern became one of the largest of its kind in the country, both as a manufacturing and distributing house." The company did a staggering amount of trade between the government of Great Britain and its colonies in silk, linen, woolen, and cotton goods.

Edith Frith Cook, Maud's mother, was born into great wealth, but this did not save her from the pain of a lonely childhood. Not just her parents but her only sister died of tuberculosis. She was raised by her father's three aunts, none of whom wanted the responsibility of mothering an orphaned girl. They sent her to boarding school, which made her so miserable that years later, when she had her own children, she made her husband promise never to send them away to school. It was the practice among the upper classes to farm out the care of their children to a nurse or governess, or to send them away to boarding school at a tender age.

When she met the dashing young Thomas Gonne, Edith's brief life took a turn for the better. They married when she was twenty-one and he was thirty, in East Peckham, Kent, near her grandfather's mansion, Roydon Hall. Tommy, as Maud called her father, came from a prosperous London family of wine merchants, but his family's fortune was small compared to that of his wife. Edith brought a dowry of £25,344 to the marriage. That's $27 million today. They were a privileged young couple. No one in either family remarked for posterity on the disparity between the two young people's fortunes, perhaps because Thomas seemed a presentable, ambitious young man on a definite, socially respectable career path.

Aged twenty-one, Gonne bought himself a position as a junior cavalry officer in the Royal Scots Greys, a regiment of the British Army. For a young man in 1846, starting out in the British cavalry must have been supremely exciting. The British Empire was then approaching the height of its military and colonial power, making it the greatest empire the world had known since Rome, over a thousand years before. As a younger son, Tommy had few choices of career. His oldest brother William had been groomed to run the family wine business, and young Tommy preferred army life, even as a junior officer, to working in his family's wine business under the thumb of his father and elder brother.

Besides, Tommy enjoyed traveling and loved languages. The army let him satisfy both his wanderlust and exercise his abilities with languages. As a young man he learned German, Portuguese, Italian, and French. In India he picked up Hindi and became the Hindustani interpreter for the regimental staff. His career serving the British Empire lasted three decades, until the end of his short life.

Maud Gonne was born December 21, 1866, in Tongham, thirty-two miles southwest of London. Tommy was stationed at the nearby Aldershot garrison. Both parents were Anglican, so Maud was christened Edith Maud Gonne in the Anglican Church in January 1867. They hired a nurse, Mary Ann Meredith, a childless young widow in her twenties, to look after Maud. "Bowie," as she was mysteriously nicknamed by the family, continued to work for Maud until the end of her long life.

In 1868 Tommy was posted to the Curragh, a military base in County Kildare, Ireland. Tommy moved his family to a suburb of Dublin, in an enclave of Anglo-Irish families, all supporters of Empire, to be close. He visited them on weekends in the house they called Floraville. The couple's second daughter, Kathleen, was born in Kildare on September 8, 1868, the only one of their two children born in Ireland.

Despite Maud Gonne's grand, lifelong passion for Ireland, she was born in England, as were her parents and grandparents. Maud claimed to be Irish through her paternal great-grandfather William Gonne who came from the Irish counties of Kerry and Mayo. William Gonne had left Ireland for Portugal, where he became a wine merchant. His descendants made their way over to London. It is through this filament of ancestry that Maud based her assertion that her father, though born in London, to British-born parents, was Irish and so was she.

When Maud arrived in Ireland as a one-year-old, Ireland was brewing new revolts against the British Empire. Fueled by Irish-American dollars and the nostalgic feelings of exiles in the US, including members of the Republican Brotherhood, founded by James Stephens, the Fenian Rising of 1867 failed. The sentiment of ardent romantic nationalism dominated Irish politics for the next one hundred years, as it had for the preceding three hundred. Like the Middle East, problems in Ireland can seem intractable because they are deeply rooted; the painful memories pass from one generation to the next.

When the Gonnes arrived, Ireland was still reeling from 1845 to 1849's Great Famine, or Great Hunger as it was also known, as if no one epitaph could adequately describe the toll of human suffering. During those years, an estimated quarter of the island's population of eight million died or emigrated. The potato crop, the staple of the diet of the Irish poor, had failed. A third of the population of Ireland depended on the potato for food, especially in the poor farming land to the rocky west. Many renters labored in the fields in exchange for rent. Ireland wasn't a cash economy. Poor renters, cottiers as they were called, had no money to buy food. Instead, they grew potatoes on their little plots, which sustained them and their families. They had no resources when the potato failed. The cottiers rented land from middlemen, employed by absentee British landlords. That system enabled the landlords to bleed the country of its cash, as, for the most part, the rents were not reinvested in the Irish properties.

Colonial administrator Charles Trevelyan, in charge of the British famine relief effort, believed like British scholar and economist Thomas Malthus that market forces should rule. In his opinion, relief should be withheld to enable market forces to work; the famine was "a mechanism for reducing surplus population." Trevelyan further declared that, "The judgement of God sent the calamity to teach the Irish a lesson, that calamity must not be too much mitigated." A common belief among the English then, in the words of noted Irish historian F. S. L. Lyons, was that "the Irish were a backward people and fundamentally unsuited for self-government." For instance, in one political cartoon they were caricatured as apelike. While sitting on the back of an English laborer, the simian creature who symbolized the Irish grinned and showed off his bag of money.

While the people starved, Irish grain and oats were shipped to England to pay their taxes, an ongoing act defended by prominent members of Parliament, including Trevelyan, who was knighted for overseeing relief works during the famine. In 1846 Trevelyan ended the soup kitchen and relief work system set up during Sir Robert Peel's administration, which had fed millions. The resulting misery, starvation, and death by fever left its mark on the Irish who survived. Today, only five percent of the eighty million members of the Irish diaspora live in Ireland; the actual population of the island, both north and south, is well below pre-famine levels. The Great Hunger's trauma lingers.

After the famine, Irish tenant farmers and nationalists agitated for fixity of tenure and rent control. Irish tenant farmers had no written lease, nor the right to one. When a rental agreement was up, usually after twelve months, they could be evicted. When evicted, they couldn't claim compensation for any improvements they had made on their farm or their land, which wasn't the case in Britain or in Ulster. The penal laws, set up by the Protestant British conquerors in the seventeenth century, made it illegal for Catholics, by far the majority of the native Irish population, to own their own land or a horse worth more than seven pounds, to enter into any of the professions, or to school their own children.

After the famine ended in 1849, demands for land reform in Ireland continued in many variations for close to ninety years. Responding to protests, public pressure within and outside of Parliament, and a huge outcry from Irish Americans, the British Government bought out the landowners at generous prices in a series of Land Acts beginning in 1870, with the last and biggest in 1903 and 1909. Then the Irish, with loans from the British government, were finally able to buy their own land in their own country. The British government required the Irish farmers to repay them, usually over a sixty-eight-year period. In 1938, on the brink of war with Germany and eager for an Irish ally, the United Kingdom agreed to cancel £100 million in repayments still outstanding for a one-time payment of £10 million by the Irish government. For the Irish, argued Joe Lee, professor emeritus of Modern History at University College Dublin and former member of the Irish Senate, this was a good deal.

In nineteenth-century Ireland, seeing—as Maud Gonne did—whole families evicted from mud-floor, thatched-roof cottages was a powerful incentive to demand political change. Thousands protested the prevailing land practices, including Maud Gonne, but until the Irish farmers owned their own land the problem continued well into the twentieth century. At age eighty-three, Maud reminisced that coming from France where she was educated, and seeing evictions in Ireland when she was a teenager, changed her from a frivolous girl who thought of little but dancing and races to a committed young activist for Ireland.

Thousands of British troops, including those serving under Thomas Gonne, who had been promoted to captain of the 17th Lancers, were garrisoned in Ireland to prevent more uprisings. Unfortunately, while his career flourished, Tommy's personal life took a turn for the worse. His wife contracted tuberculosis. Consumption, as it was then called, was also known as "the white plague" because of the victim's shocking pallor. This infectious and often fatal disease attacks the lungs and throat, and via the bloodstream can spread throughout the body. In the nineteenth century it was also called the *mal de siè-cle*, the sickness of the century. Tuberculosis remains a worldwide scourge, as strains ever more resistant to antibiotics evolve. (In 2016 it was the world's number one cause of death from infectious disease, beating out AIDS for that dubious distinction.) Before the discovery of antibiotics, it was usually fatal. In 1851 an estimated one in four deaths in Europe and America were due to TB. Both of Edith's parents died of it, and they were a statistic.

Ill with a slow, wasting disease, suffering from a sore throat and a deep cough, Edith was pregnant for the third time in the spring of 1871 when she, the girls, and Bowie moved to London. They stayed with her aunt and looked for a house where Tommy could join them. One was found at 63 Gloucester Terrace, near Hyde Park, and that is where she died on June 22, 1871, one week after the birth of her baby girl Margaretta Rose. The baby, who didn't outlive her mother for long, died five weeks later and is buried near Edith in the Tongham Church graveyard. Tommy, who had taken leave from his regiment to be with his wife, was devastated.

In her memoir, Maud Gonne recalls the spooky scene when at four years old she learned that her mother was dead. It was morning:

> I had gone to find Mama. My small fumbling fingers suc-
> ceeded in turning the handle of the door of her room; I
> was afraid nurse would catch me before I got it open. The
> room was dark and lit by candles although it was daylight.
> Tommy was kneeling by the bed. As I opened the door he
> turned his head. He was crying. Harshly he said: "Go away,"
> and nurse, coming down the stairs, captured me.

When the men were waiting to carry down the coffin, her father fetched her to "say good-bye to Mama."

Unable to continue on in the house where he had lived with his wife, Tommy moved the children and their nurse to the camp at Curragh, where he was stationed. Then the motherless girls moved with Bowie to Howth, a fishing village east of Dublin. A peninsula forming the northern arm of Dublin Bay, Howth is surrounded by the sea and has a glorious coastline. Tommy joined them on weekends. Given his demanding career in the British Army, he could not be the modern model of the stay-at-home dad.

Maud Gonne's complicated issues with men began with her affectionate, appealing but unavailable father. He worked throughout the British Empire, from Austria to Russia, Africa, and India as a military officer and diplomat. Maud idolized him. In reality she had no single caring adult in a position of responsibility looking after her and her sister on a daily basis, apart from Bowie. We don't know much about Bowie, except that she was "a sociable soul," and a healer who earned a positive reputation in the little community. In her memoir Maud writes much more about her father than she does her nurse, who lived with her until she was a young woman of twenty-one and played a key role in her life.

Maud speculates in her memoir that a doctor recommended a more appealing climate for her as a little girl; the fear was that, like her mother, she was tubercular. In that era tuberculosis was believed to be hereditary, which it is not. However, even as an adult Maud remained highly susceptible to the deep, racking coughs of bronchitis and feared that she might develop the disease that had been fatal to so many members of her family.

Howth is a romantic, lovely place, redolent with history. Even now on the Dart—the electric rail that runs there from Dublin despite the spread of the city—you can watch seals play in the sea, just by the station. Their dark heads and big moist eyes bob up from the water, charming visitors on the dark sand and black rock beach. One hundred and fifty years ago it must have been even more secluded and wild.

A Norman castle dating back to the twelfth century stands on the Howth peninsula. It has been the home of the St. Lawrence family for eight hundred years. Five centuries later a legend about the castle lingers. In 1576 the pirate Gráinne Ní Mháille—Grace O'Malley—is said to have tried to visit the Earl of Howth, Nicholas St. Lawrence, at the castle at dinnertime. She expected to be invited in for supper and obtain supplies for her voyage back to her home in the west. He rebuffed her, breaking the ancient Irish code of hospitality to strangers, whether or not those strangers were outlaws. He left the castle gates closed. Furious, the pirate queen kidnapped the Earl's grandson and heir, Christopher St. Lawrence. Her ransom demand? That the Earl promise uninvited guests never again be turned away, that the gates of his park should always remain open. An extra place, she insisted, must be set for surprise visitors in the formal dining room. To this day, an extra place is laid at Howth Castle.

The legend is in keeping with the nationwide tradition of Irish hospitality, both north and south. It is said that strangers should never be turned away from a house at night, as they might be descendants of the Celtic lords, Catholics who were dispossessed of their land by the Protestant Queen Elizabeth of England in the sixteenth century. What had been a territorial war between Ireland and England became a Catholic versus Protestant war, one Christian faith set against another. According to folklore, in the seventeenth century the dreaded Oliver Cromwell, Lord Protector of the British Isles, had no compunction about offering the defeated Irish lords the choice of "To hell or to Connaught!" Cromwell and other Protestants believed that when Catholics were killed without renouncing their faith first, they went straight to hell. Connaught is a rocky poor province in the west of Ireland. The choice before the conquered Irish was to give up their land and move west—or die.

As a child, Maud would have heard this story. In Howth, her nurse made friends with the locals on her way to and from the post office. By saving a sick baby she had earned a reputation for nursing and healing. Eggs, buttermilk, and mushrooms were given to Bowie in return for her ointments, powders, and freely given time. An added bonus: the nurse and girls were invited in for tea, griddle cake, and potatoes by their neighbors. In one of their homes Maud would likely have learned the legend of the intrepid Celtic pirate queen. The pictures the child saw on the walls were of Irish rebels: Wolfe Tone, Robert Emmet, and Michael Larkin, side by side with paintings of the Blessed Virgin and the family's favorite Irish saints. In Ireland, Maud was quietly absorbing a revolutionary Catholic belief system, quite different from that of her family's Anglican values.

Maud loved Howth. "No place has ever seemed as lovely to me as Howth was then," she remembered. "Sometimes the sea was as blue as Mama's turquoises ... The little rock pools at the bottom of the high cliffs were full of wonder-life; sea-anemones which open look like gorgeous flowers with blue and orange spots and, if touched, close up into ugly brown lumps, tiny crabs, pink star-fish, endless varieties of sea-snails." Bowie took them to bathe in the shallow pools and clamber on the cliffs. Maud remembered hiding in the heather. The children were allowed to play all day long. They had no formal lessons except the ones Tommy gave them on weekends in reading, writing, and arithmetic.

Their unschooled Irish idyll came to an end after Tommy attended a luncheon at the castle home of Lord St. Lawrence of Howth, the same castle where the pirate queen is said to have been turned away centuries before. Tommy brought his little girls. A society woman at lunch criticized Tommy for letting his children run around wild without a governess. Soon after, Tommy hired an English governess, the daughter of a vicar, to educate his girls. A Miss Bromley, in Maud's words: "A kindly stupid woman who did her best, but as she herself had only a smattering of the wide knowledge she was supposed to impart we learned very little from her."

In 1874 Tommy was assigned to Aldershot, England. The girls and Bowie were shipped off to their mother's aunt in London. Great-Aunt Augusta was married to the Reverend Thomas Tarleton. Neither seemed to like children. The children, for their part, hated the big, dark cold formal house in Hyde Park Gardens, where they were waited on by eight servants. When seven-year-old Maud heard that they were leaving, she danced in front of the big mirror on the first landing, singing:

Hooray, hooray, hooray!
Today we are going away.

The next relative's house she and her sister were dropped into was the home of their great-uncle Frank in Richmond, outside London. Son of the vastly wealthy William Cook, Francis had a renowned art collection that included Rembrandt, Dürer, Van Dyck, and El Greco. He had built two galleries to accommodate his expensive tastes. The children liked this home better than Aunt Augusta's. They could run up and down the gallery halls and play in the winter garden that featured exotic palms and bamboo. Their father visited and kept in touch by letter. To his "little lamb"—Maud's nickname—he wrote before her birthday on December 21:

> I do so wish I was with you to help make this birthday go off well and see your pretty tree. I know you will be so happy because this year, no doubt, you are more good than last. When you have ended rejoicing over your own birthday, another glorious day will arrive in the same week, which is a birthday kept by everyone, rich and poor. I know Miss Bromley will let you know and understand why Xmas day makes everyone so happy ... How pleased I shall be to hear how your party goes off. Will you let that Old Bear wear a crown. I think you both had one on her birthday. Make "Nan" wear her new dress and thank Miss Bromley for her note.... Be so good and all must be gay!
>
> Your own Dad,
> T. Gonne

In the spring of 1876, their doting if absent father was appointed military attaché to the court of Emperor Franz Joseph of Austria. Maud was nine and Kathleen seven. That posting lasted for two years. The devoted Bowie was always with the girls, the one constant in their young lives, besides their father's steady stream of letters and visits.

From Vienna he sent "Lamb" a letter on July 12: "I am every day expecting a charming letter for your continuing good marks from the past week." He told her about the Shah of Persia's visit and other entertaining details of his life in Vienna, closing:

Hug our Bow and Bear (for) me
Your loving Dad
T. Gonne

Bear was his nickname for Kathleen, who was thought to be more like their mother, very good-natured in contrast to the strong-willed, hard to control Maud. The braver and bigger girl was called Lamb because of her long, spindly legs while the docile, soft little sister was called Bear—ironic, considering how their lives unfolded.

In the fall Tommy marched into Bosnia as military attaché of the Third Army Corps of the Austrian Army. The Bosnians were in revolt against Austrian annexation. For his service to the Austro-Hungarian Empire, Tommy won the Austrian War Medal and was promoted to lieutenant colonel. In October 1878 he was allowed leave to return home to his girls.

While he'd been away, the children had stayed with yet another relative, Tommy's older brother Charles, his wife, and their five children in Ascot, twenty-five miles west of London. The sisters had become especially close to their female cousins Chotie (Catherine) and May (Mary), who were six and four years older than Maud. The Ascot mansion was surrounded by shrubbery, which Maud recalled in her memoir as being "gloomy."

Maud remembered that after her mother's death, her father had taken her aside and told her: "You must never be afraid of anything, not even of death." That advice guided her throughout her life. As a little girl at her uncle's home in Ascot, she forced herself to walk alone in the dark shrubbery without the company of her cousins or sister: "At first I ran all the time and was breathless when I reached the house, but I took the fearsome walk every night till I could do it slowly and without a tremor."

Maud would deliberately challenge herself as a child so that she wouldn't be afraid when she grew up. Even situations that frightened grown men apparently didn't interfere with her love for action. If her father inspired Maud to challenge herself, she never mentioned it in her memoirs. Perhaps her father's example, winning medals for bravery in faraway places, was enough to make her try to emulate him.

On a lighter note, the Ascot races were nearby. The fashionable, horse-loving Gonne family probably attended, perhaps cheering on Silvio, the champion British thoroughbred who won three races at Ascot between 1874 and 1879, and in 1878 earned more than any other English horse.

In 1879, the 17th Lancers joined British troops for another colonial war in what is now South Africa. Tommy was the commander. War had broken out between the Zulus and the British. An accident—Tommy shot himself in the thigh while cleaning his pistol—resulted in his being sent home to England for close to a year. The girls were delighted to have their father with them. But the demands of his career were relentless, and that summer Tommy was ordered to join the Lancers in India.

Before leaving he rented a villa in the south of France and engaged a French governess for his girls. Maud was twelve and a half, Kathleen had just turned eleven. An English doctor had recommended Tommy send his daughters to the sunny Riviera because the climate was thought to be good for Maud's health. Medical geography—going to warm, dry places for one's health—had become popular in the United States and in Europe by the second half of the nineteenth century. The improved climate and dry air were thought especially healing for consumptives.

For Tommy, avoiding the cold, damp English winters was a positive solution to Maud's worrisome pulmonary troubles. The children loved their villa on the road between Cannes and Grasse. The Villa Fleurie had mimosa, orange, and lemon trees and violets on its grounds. The profusion of flowers remained a vivid memory for Maud years later.

Her father hired Mademoiselle Deployant to give the children French lessons. She was the first educator to make an indelible impression on the young adolescent. Maud called Mademoiselle "a strong Republican." In the Third Republic, after the French defeat in the Franco–Prussian War and the loss of Alsace-Lorraine, being a strong Republican in France could mean several different things, as demonstrated by the complicated views of grown-up Maud. One could belong to reform-minded France as an heir to the French Revolution, or one could see oneself as patriot and a nationalist, more than a republican. Nationalists prided themselves on being supporters of the Army and the Church, and many yearned for a new Napoleonic leader to emerge and recover France's past glory. These were among the beliefs that Maud digested as a young woman.

In her memoir, Maud doesn't distinguish between these different colored threads in the vibrant shifting tapestry of nineteenth-century French politics. Perhaps her Mademoiselle, an independent woman who never married and saved up enough money to live on her own in a villa with a dog named Toutou and a cat named Catichat, belonged to the *liberté, egalité, fraternité* type of French Republicans. Maud remembered that Mademoiselle encouraged her charges to be independent. She doesn't specify if that meant emotional, intellectual, financial independence, or all three, but Mademoiselle was one of three adult women role models for young Maud. The first was her nurse, the second Mademoiselle. Maud wrote that through Mademoiselle she learned to find and appreciate beauty wherever she saw it:

> She succeeded in making us love our lessons and find them as exciting as play; she taught us history, some would say with a republican bias, but it was human history and she taught us to love human beings and to love beauty and to see it everywhere. . . . She had given us the desire to learn;

she made us love literature and took the trouble to discuss it with us.

Tommy left his girls at Villa Fleurie in the hands of Bowie and Mademoiselle and travelled to India. For the following six years, his children lived abroad, in Switzerland in the winter, Italy or the South of France during the summer. Whenever he had leave, Tommy went to meet them, and then they travelled together as if it were a holiday. He wrote them chatty, warm letters from his various postings. From India: "It is such a pleasure to know the extreme cold of England doesn't reach Cannes. Tell Bowie I'm sure she would have suffered in London."

From the Volga in Russia he wrote his Lamb: "You must not run any risk this year then we may expect you to outgrow your chest weakness that made you so ill last winter. Now is the time to take special care on the principle that a stitch in time saves a doctor's bill."

Tommy sent presents: furs from Russia, a watch, money for new clothes. He was as involved as he could be in his children's upbringing, asking the girls to keep up with their lessons, to work on their French, and promising to get them a French cook so they could all speak French together when he came home.

Despite his best efforts, the girls had a peripatetic childhood. Maud's complicated issues around men began with her having an affectionate, doting father who because of his work as soldier and diplomat was often gone. In his absence she idolized him, an idolization made even more acute because she had no mother. In their six years travelling on the continent and in England, the Gonne sisters grew up. Maud's early attachment to Ireland may have developed because in Ireland she saw her father every weekend and she and her sister ran around freely with the local children.

By fourteen, Maud was five feet, ten inches tall. She looked sophisticated and tried to hurry into adulthood: "Having a great desire to be grown up, I made Nurse lengthen my skirts and dress the masses of my gold-brown hair in great coils at the back of my head. Tommy looked amazingly young." According to Maud, "more and more he treated me as a companion." Maud was amused that when on an excursion together "people would take us for a honeymoon couple." It all seems very much to be an Electra complex, a daughter vying with her mother for her father's attention. Maud seems never to have resolved this first crush with a more realistic appraisal of the man who was her father.

When Maud was sixteen in 1883, her father returned from his posting to Russia. There is no record of his next posting for a few years. While Maud was a teenager, he introduced her to Paris and to her great-aunt Mary, the Countess of Sizeranne, who had "an exquisite little flat hung with red damask." The stylish countess was the third female role model for young Maud. Her great-aunt's second marriage had been to the Count Paul Ange Henri Monier de La Sizeranne. The multitalented count had served in the Second Empire as a deputy and as a senator. He wrote plays. His wife was equally sophisticated. When Maud met her "Aunt Mary," as she called the regal old beauty, she had buried two husbands and kept a much younger lover on a string. She called him her "secretary." At seventy, she wore black velvet and kept her beautiful white hair high up on her head in a do that resembled Marie Antoinette's. It wasn't a wig, according to Maud, who once tried to comb and dress it when her aunt's French maid took ill and recalled failing miserably. Aunt Mary's devoted young "secretary" was named Figlio. Sometimes she and her secretary quarreled, then Figlio would send roses and they'd make up. Passionate sex presumably followed.

An important lesson Aunt Mary taught her impressionable great-niece was that it didn't matter how ugly the men in her life were, but "women must be beautiful." As she demonstrated in her own person, that took work. Under the tutelage of her aunt, Maud learned the importance of beauty and of good presentation of one's hair, makeup, and dress. More importantly, Maud, like her seventy-year-old aunt, learned to use beauty to manipulate men and get them to do as she wanted. One of Aunt Mary's hobbies was launching beauties into European society. Introduced to the willowy teenager, the Countess realized Maud could be a great success in high society. She begged Tommy to leave the girl in her care. However, while visiting her aunt on holiday in Homburg, Germany "at a fashionable hotel," Maud attracted the attention of the Prince of Wales. Her delighted aunt expected an invitation to supper, but Tommy swooped in and took Maud away with him to the opera in Bayreuth. He batted away interested suitors because he felt she was too young to marry. Nor did he want her to be a mistress, despite the Countess introducing Maud to the demimonde in the person of her young "secretary," and despite his letting the Countess train Maud in the arts of a courtesan in the city where such women were celebrated and memorialized in literature. The intelligent and sophisticated among the beauties and the courtesans ran their own salons.

On one of their visits to Paris, Maud spent an afternoon with the Countess. On that storied visit, remembered fifty years later, Maud and her aunt took a drive in a carriage in the Bois de Boulogne. They went to the perfumers where Aunt Mary advised her great-niece, "You should always use the same perfume, one that suits you." Maud paid attention and used a recognizable perfume as an adult, so much so that this scent crept into one of her admirer's dreams. Next Aunt Mary took Maud to a hat shop where she bought her grand-niece a fashionable, large black lace hat. Aunt Mary's was an education of a different sort than Mademoiselle's, one that Maud was to draw on for the rest of her life. No matter where she lived, Maud's clothes and, later, the fabric for the black dress and veil she habitually wore when she returned to Ireland in 1918, came from Paris.

Chapter 2
An Irish Debutante Takes a French Lover

In 1885 Tommy, aged fifty, took the post of assistant adjutant general in Ireland, making him second-in-command of British armed forces in Ireland. When he accepted that position, he established a new residence in Dublin, and Maud, Kathleen, and Bowie moved in with him. Maud began to act as hostess for her father. She was anxious to prove she could run his household. At twenty, he regularly brought her with him on social occasions, including to balls, and sometimes she was mistaken for his wife. This pleased Maud, who had been in such a hurry to grow up as a teenager. The winter after they moved to Dublin, the Gonne sisters made their formal debut, no doubt thrilling the formidable Countess, their great-aunt Mary.

During the social season at Dublin Castle (the seat of the British military and civilian government in Ireland) the two teens engaged in a heady whirl of parties. British military officers and their wives, daughters, and sons dined with local Anglo-Irish families. Engagements were made and broken. Royalty attended the parties. Prince Edward of Saxe-Weimar came to Dublin for the Saint Patrick's Day ball. Prince Albert Victor, son of the Prince of Wales, came to the Dublin Castle ball and danced with Maud.

It is difficult to know if Maud was naturally theatrical and loved costumes, or if she learned to pay meticulous attention to her outfits and her grooming from her impeccably turned out great-aunt. For one debutante party, Maud wore a green velvet gown adorned with white flowers. For another, she wore a ball dress of white satin, decorated with gauze petals embroidered on the train, designed by her to look as if she were emerging from water lilies swirling around her feet. She had imagination, stature, and an appealing speaking voice. Maud became the "Belle of the Season."

While living in Dublin she had a leisurely routine. Mornings she went riding with her sister in Phoenix Park, a green refuge in the middle of the city. Twice the size of New York City's Central Park, Phoenix Park remains delightful, with walking, hiking trails, and bicycle lanes. In 1885, when the Gonne sisters rode through the park, it was grand, green countryside with grazing deer. Like Tommy, Maud loved horses and had several favorites, one an old charger of her father's named Yellow Jack. Evenings she and her sister Kathleen fulfilled social obligations with their widowed father.

However, Maud wasn't oblivious to what went on beyond the gaiety of the social life revolving around Dublin Castle. In an interview given in 1950, three years before she died, Maud remembered:

> It was the eviction I saw in 1885, after I returned from France where I was educated, which changed the whole course of my life, changing me from a frivolous girl who thought of little but dancing and race meetings, into a woman of fixed purpose—to help our Mother (Ireland) get the stranger out of her home.

She had been invited to a hunt ball in the Midlands region. Trying to make small talk with her host who was busy eating, she asked him about hunting. To her surprise, he began ranting to her about the Land League, whose members agitated for fair rent, fixity of tenure, and free sale of their renting rights:

> "They would stop us hunting. . . . As I was coming home this evening, I saw Paddy Ward and his family lying out

in a ditch [because he had been evicted for nonpayment of rent]. His wife doesn't look as if she was going to live til morning, I told him he would be responsible for her death. I had warned him as to what would happen if he joined the Land League. Now he has no roof to shelter his family and the woman will be dead before tomorrow."

"And you did nothing about it?"

"Let her die." He answered. "These people must be taught a lesson," and he went on eating his dinner.

That night Maud sent a telegram to her father, asking him to have a carriage meet her at the railway station in the morning. Appalled by her host's hard heart, she went home. In her father, Maud had found an ally—he didn't object to her abrupt departure—and, she claimed, a role model for the Irish political advocate she was to become. Looking back at seventy, it was important for her to state that her father and she were on the same page. According to her memoir, he objected to the English treatment of the conquered Irish and planned to quit his job with the British army and run for Parliament as an Irish Home Rule candidate. Then he died. So, Maud wasn't able to undertake this important work with her father as she dreamed of doing.

Whether or not this was actually true, it was central to the myth that Maud constructed, one among many that she used to launch herself into the world of international politics. She saw herself as spokesperson for "Mother Ireland." Did the orphaned young woman find an emotional and political anchor in the image of a mystical Mother, who needed Maud's written, vocal, and performance skills to make the rest of the world know about the evils the Mother suffered under British colonial law? That could be one reason young Maud took up the cause of Ireland. It gave her an emotional home: a reason to live besides fulfilling the social obligations that came with the giddy life of a sought-after debutante.

Proving Maud's claim about her father's intentions is impossible. He died at fifty-one and left no written record of his politics. Having spent his entire adult life in the service of the British Empire, his taking a political stand divergent from the majority of Englishmen seems unlikely. On the other hand, having seen the miserable reality of Irish life while stationed in Ireland for eight years, he may have gradually become convinced of the rightness of Home Rule as a means to improve the Irish people's lot. Home Rulers believed the passage of the bill would quell the need for armed rebellion in Ireland and incidentally save the British the expense of deploying thousands of troops to the hostile neighboring island.

Had Tommy taken this path, he would have been following in the footsteps of his former commanding officer, Lord Lieutenant of Ireland, John Spencer, Fifth Earl Spencer, whose descendant was Lady Diana Spencer, Princess of Wales. The earl had been appointed lord lieutenant by British Prime Minister William Gladstone, serving from 1868–74 and 1882–1885. Those appointments made him chief of British armed forces in Ireland.

Spencer gradually moved to a much more radical position than his fellow MPs, a position at odds with the redoubtable Gladstone. Presumably his views were affected by the time he spent in Ireland, running the country for Britain. Spencer believed the British government should set up overseers to enforce fair, fixed rents for the Irish peasantry. Tommy, an intelligent Englishman, could have modeled his wish to be a radical Home Rule MP on Lord Spencer's lonesome political stand in the British Parliament. However, instead of fulfilling Maud's dream of working together to rescue Ireland, Tommy died on November 30, 1886 of typhoid fever, ten years before German doctors invented a vaccine. What Tommy's doctor had dismissed as an inconsequential fever turned out to be the dreaded international fever, spread by a bacillus, often through unsanitary water or food conditions of which there were plenty in nineteenth-century Dublin. Before the invention of new medical technology, typhoid fever was difficult to distinguish from milder fevers because scientists had not yet invented ways to identify the specific bacteria that caused it.

After his death, Tommy's two devastated daughters, along with the faithful Bowie, were sent to live with yet another relative. The girls had to pack up their home and move in with Tommy's bachelor brother William, the oldest of the Gonne siblings, who ran the family wine business out of their London office, like his father and grandfather. Tommy had appointed William their guardian and he took his executor role seriously, keeping a tight hold on their inheritance. Not only were the girls anguished by the sudden death of their beloved father, they had to leave behind their gay life in Dublin and live with their miserly uncle in London. He not only kept them on a small allowance of half a crown a week (less than a dollar today), unlike their generous, high-living father who regularly sent them both gifts and money, Uncle William gave them ledgers to record their weekly expenses. He asked to see them each Saturday. In her memoirs, Maud laughed at him and confessed to neatly writing down her expenses in advance. She made them up.

Almost twenty years after the death of Charles Dickens, the London of 1887 to which the girls moved arguably remained a dreary, gloomy yet bustling city. Dickens's title "Hard Times" applied to the majority of the working English poor in their newly industrialized country. They lived desperately in cramped dark slums. Factories developed during Britain's Industrial Revolution created "smog"—a neologism for the lethal combination of thick black chimney smoke and London's famous pea-soup fog. Factories were dismal places to work, without laws to protect people's safety. Many were hurt without being compensated. There were no child labor laws, no laws to limit the hours children or their parents worked. Trafalgar Square, the Houses of Parliament, and Victoria Station were all built during the Victorian era by the industrious British poor. This was the London to which the Gonne sisters moved.

London was a cauldron of new political and artistic ideas. Maud, an intellectually curious young woman, probably learned about the more radical ideas circulating there, as surely as she breathed in her first breaths of smog. The socialist playwright George Bernard Shaw and the revolutionary Karl Marx lived in London when the Gonne sisters arrived. 1887 was the year of Queen Victoria's Jubilee. Alfred Lord Tennyson was poet laureate of England and Ireland from 1850 to 1892, his post ending upon his death. However, beneath the majestic veneer of empire, there were rumblings. Massive changes were to come. In 1889 Emmeline Pankhurst founded the Women's Franchise League to win suffrage for married women. She became more radical as she aged, petitioning for all women to have the right to vote. The Fabian society voiced the demands of labor, specifically of the disenfranchised working class. In 1887 anarchists, opposed to the entire industrial and political organization of their countries, began to outnumber socialists in the Socialist League in London formed a few years prior. It seemed as the century drew to a close, more and more people were getting radicalized in London.

Maud was a witness to some of the roiling unrest. She heard speeches and participated in demonstrations. On February 12, 1886, some ten thousand unemployed men congregated in Trafalgar Square and, according to Maud, her uncle William forbade her to leave the house. Gleefully, she disobeyed. Already, at age twenty, she had an instinct for finding political action hot spots. She could more easily relate to the poor working class, rather than to her prosperous, conservative uncle. At the Trafalgar Square protest Maud met Tom Mann, the controversial English leader of the Socialist Democratic Federation, a party whose members included Friedrich Engels. Engels and Marx developed the hugely influential communist doctrine that was to literally change the world. Mann invited Maud down to the platform to speak, but she said no. Instead, from her safe position up high, she watched bobbies swing into action, followed by rioting and beatings. Then the crowd moved on and smashed shop windows. Throughout her life, rather than being frightened by demonstrations, Maud reveled in them. Her childhood fortitude exercises gave her more courage than many grown men and women who were well aware of the possibility of being crushed.

Meanwhile, Maud's unhappiness in her uncle's home continued. The house was located at 11 St. Helen's Street near a large, famous, and conservative Anglican church. The church had more monuments than any London church apart from Westminster Abbey. Uncle William regularly attended, even on cold winter Sunday mornings, and he expected his wards to accompany him. Perhaps Maud's body responded to the stress of being an orphan in a hostile, if privileged, environment. Or perhaps her active body, as well as her spirit, rebelled against the punishing stricture of nineteenth-century whalebone corsets as well as the damp cold winter air of London. She became ill with pneumonia. Her cousins May and Chotie tried to cheer her up.

William, alarmed at Maud's independent ways and her political views, which clashed with the interest of the Anglican governing class, lied to his grieving wards. He told the girls their inheritance was gone because of Tommy's mismanagement. He hoped this lie would clip their troublesome wings. Without money of their own, the girls had few choices: to be William's dependents until they married, to become rich old society ladies' paid companions, or else to be governesses to children of the wealthy. Since their education was spotty, they probably could not even have been governesses. Women had few options in 1886, when the girls moved into William's home. As Bernard Shaw memorably showed in *Pygmalion*, the play adapted as *My Fair Lady*, an educated, well-spoken young girl of that era was really fit for little except the marriage market.

Maud's response outraged Uncle William. She had dabbled in amateur theatricals in Dublin. Actresses then had to provide their own wardrobe, an advantage for Maud who, courtesy of her aunt and her father's good taste, had fabulous dresses from Paris. Once she was in London, the theatrical capital of the English-speaking world, Maud became interested in performing professionally. A smart woman as well as a beauty, she used her looks and her voice to become a professional actress. She told the scandalized William that was how she would support herself going forward. Maud had proof she could do so. She had auditioned for a local touring company and landed the leading role. Shocked, Uncle William revealed to his wards that they had a sizable inheritance. Tommy left £28,828 to his daughters. Once they each turned twenty-one, £14,414 (roughly $2 million each) was theirs to spend as they saw fit. Neither would ever have to make a living by becoming a companion, a wife, or worse in William's eyes, a professional actress. If Uncle William wished to control the two sisters' behavior while they lived with him in his bachelor home, he had failed.

Despite his strenuous objections, Maud refused to quit her first acting job. During rehearsals for the play *Heartsease*, Maud began to cough. The vocal work she was doing to train her voice had strained it. Determined not to give up her first big role, Maud continued with rehearsals. The play is the translation of the French drama *Adrienne Lecouvreur* by Eugène Scribe and Ernest Legouvé, based on the life of the titular celebrated eighteenth-century actress, the tragic tale of Adrienne Lecouvreur. Lecouvreur was a friend of Voltaire and the lover of the Comte Maurice de Saxe. Aged twenty-eight and at the height of her fame, she died. Rumor had it she was poisoned by a jealous rival. As if prescient, Maud had chosen for her first starring role a play about a beautiful young woman who achieved notoriety in her own time, much as Maud was to do in hers.

Rehearsals continued; Maud's cough got worse, and she coughed up blood. Alarmed, Maud's doctor directed his patient to go south, out of chill, dank London to a thermal hot springs spa in a warmer climate. Her great-aunt Mary stepped in and whisked Maud and her sister Kathleen off to Royat in central France. The spa was well-known because it had been used by the Emperor Napoleon III and his wife, the Empress Eugénie. More than a century after the Gonne women visited, the thermal spa of Royat continues to tout treatment for illnesses as varied as fibromyalgia, arthritis, and heart disease.

In 1886, when the Gonne women traveled down to Royat from Paris, it was the fashion—begun in the early nineteenth century in the United States and Europe—to heal at a "sanitarium," a word used to describe many spas. Business was booming. Typically built in sunny climes with cool dry air—high up in the mountains of Switzerland, in and around Denver, Colorado, and in the Adirondacks—sanatoria were thought to improve the functioning of the heart and respiratory system and to stop the progression of that international killer of millions, tuberculosis. Rest, high altitude, fresh air, and good food were all believed to help cure infection of the lungs. Historian Gregg Mitman has described these health sojourns made possible by the invention of the steam locomotive as the "geography of hope":

> Sufferers seek hope—medicine trades upon it. . . . Climate, air, and sunshine were marketable health commodities, sold by railroads, civic boosters, and physicians to consumptives and asthmatics looking for relief, if not a cure.

Royat is in the Auvergne region of France, high up from a flat plain near the pleasantly busy, small city Clermont-Ferrand. About a half-day's hike up from Royat is the majestic volcano Puy de Dôme. It shows the rift created by the formation of the Alps thirty-five million years ago. Hikers can find the ruins of a Roman temple dedicated to Mercury, the quick-witted, fleet messenger of the gods, on top of the small mountain. The Puy de Dôme is almost a mile high and is located in the middle of a chain of eighty dormant volcanoes.

Nestled near the base of the Puy de Dôme, Royat is a beautiful small town of some five thousand people, filled with gracious nineteenth-century buildings and hotels from the Belle Époque in pastel colors, soft whites, and yellows. The thermal baths located in the center of Royat were built in 1854 by the French architect Agis-Léon Ledru, in the classical style. Stone women in deceptively simple-looking Roman shifts adorn the summit of the pillars in front of the thermal baths and lead gullible visitors to believe they are entering a special, curative haven. To a skeptical visitor, it seems designed to lull one into the belief that here in this ancient, appealing town you can find a soothing cure for what ails you.

In his novel *Mont-Oriol, or, A Romance of Auvergne*, Guy de Maupassant writes about French spa villages where, removed from their everyday life, people go on long walks after their treatments, dream of healing, and fall in love. That is what happened to Maud. Aged twenty, orphaned, searching for meaning and a larger purpose in life, the beautiful young convalescent was ripe for love. The spa town of Royat provided a charming backdrop for Maud to fall for the Frenchman who became her lover for twelve years, Lucien Millevoye.

Chapter 3
An Irish Nationalist Star Is Born

Sixteen years Maud's senior with a full head of dark hair and impressive waxed mustache, Lucien Millevoye cuts a distinguished figure in photographs. He was tall, like Maud. Also like Maud he came from an educated, respected family, and was at the spa for his health. Lucien was likely more experienced sexually: he was married, with a son, and separated from his wife Adrienne. His grandfather Charles was a well-known poet, and of course poets had an abiding appeal for Maud. In Paris, Lucien distinguished himself as a local magistrate, or judge, and as a contributor of right-wing, nationalist articles to one of the first popular newspapers sold on the streets of Paris, *La Presse*.

Millevoye was a staunch supporter of Georges Ernest Boulanger—Général Revanche—former French minister of war. Millevoye hoped the popular general would run France, win back Alsace-Lorraine from the Prussians, and return his country to Napoleonic glory. Boulanger had a beloved mistress in Royat named Marguerite Bonnemains, a vicomtesse. That was one reason Millevoye went to Royat: to see his hero, who was trysting with his mistress. Boulanger's mistress ran a famous local restaurant hotel called La Belle Meunière. When Maud first visited the restaurant, it was in the company of Lucien, the vicomtesse, and Boulanger, which must have been exciting for Maud, who loved intrigue. She wrote: "Some diplomacy had to be exercised to avoid Aunt Mary.... A lucky excursion to the mountains . . . to which we were invited, provided the occasion; I said the excursion was too tiring for me and Aunt

Mary never heard of the dinner at 'la Belle Meunière's' and of my meeting General Boulanger."

At Royat, Lucien could accomplish many goals: plot with his adored general, seek spa treatments for his health, and have the pleasure of seducing a young beauty. Maud, staying at a grand hotel nearby with Kathleen and Mary, must have been very lightly chaperoned. In the past, her great-aunt Mary had encouraged Maud's admirers, so long as the men were attractive, rich, titled aristocrats. Kathleen no doubt wanted to cheer her older sister up. Both were recovering from the sudden death of their youthful father six months before. The smooth, courteous Frenchman certainly gave Maud something to think about other than her father and the constant worry about her lungs.

When she first saw him, she and her party were sitting on the promenade, fanning themselves. The drama of a gathering thunderstorm unfolded in the sky above, and she spoke first. "I kept wondering where I had met him before. At last I asked him." "But no, mademoiselle, it is impossible," he adroitly replied to la belle Maud. "I would never have forgotten if I had met you."

As an heiress in control of her own fortune, she was in the singular position of being able to break tradition and make the first move—although making the first move had its own tradition among highborn British women. In the seventeenth-century play *The Duchess of Malfi*, the beautiful Duchess, as imagined by John Webster, woos a good-hearted man beneath her high station to the displeasure of her conniving elder brothers. Her siblings want to use her as a pawn in an international game of power politics and marriage. Since she disobeys, her two older brothers hire a man to murder the newlyweds. In real life, Elizabeth I of England disdained marriage, preferring to keep her sovereignty, her fortune, and her body. Called the Virgin Queen, she chose lovers rather than a husband. So it seemed, for a good decade of her life, did Maud.

Perhaps being an orphan and independently wealthy emboldened Maud to speak first to the tall attractive stranger. In her book
Motherless Daughters, Hope Edelman, who lost her own mother as
a girl and spent years interviewing motherless daughters, writes of
the aching emptiness such loss can create in a sensitive girl with no
grown-up female to provide her with daily affection and or a role
model. In Maud's peripatetic life, where could she go for constant
physical affection except to her nurse Bowie and her sister Kathleen?
Their absent, but amusing father created yet another void in the life
of his treasured girls.

As they talked, she found Millevoye's patriotism and commitment to French nationalism exciting. A political player in French politics, he had allied himself with the Catholic clergy, the Bonapartists,
and the army. His concern was to keep France safe from anarchists
and relics of the Paris Commune, the socialist elected government
of Paris, crushed by the army in 1871. Lucien wanted France to regain
its military supremacy in Europe and in North Africa. His dream was
to see France become the most important power in Europe, and once
again surpass England's empire, as it had done under Napoleon.

Lucien and Maud took walks in the foothills of the Puy de Dôme
and discussed politics and, one imagines, love. Perhaps in the magical atmosphere of that pretty little spa town, they didn't need to do
so explicitly. In *Mont-Oriol*, de Maupassant describes the ease into
which one could slip into amour at fashionable spas. Millevoye, older
and more experienced, could guide the young idealist in her career
path as well as guide her in love. He bluntly told Maud her talents
would be wasted on the stage. An actress would soon be forgotten by
history, he insisted. Why didn't she turn herself into "the Irish Joan
of Arc" instead? Why didn't she use her looks, her charisma, and her
distinctive voice to help free Ireland from the clutches of the British
Empire?

In her discreet memoir, she describes how "an alliance" between
the two lovers first formed, opting for a geopolitical term for their

amorous relationship. Lucien argued that together they could help their two countries fight Germany and England and so restore glory to France and liberate Ireland. The idea of ending Ireland's political and economic servitude to Great Britain set Maud on fire. "England," Lucien told Maud, "is [also] the hereditary enemy of France."

"Now we speak the same language," said Gonne, with her hands in his. "I accept this alliance, this pact against the British Empire and it is a pact to death."

From the start, Maud's passion for a man was entwined with politics. Written in the Victorian Era, Maud's memoir never mentions that her alliance with Lucien included sex. One hopes she fell utterly in love with the older, urbane experienced Frenchman, who offered her a role other than the boring one of being an aristocrat or officer's wife. Lucien gave the heartbroken young woman a vision of a life dedicated to a grand, important cause on the world stage.

Her lover's suggestion appealed to Maud. As an Irish Joan of Arc, she realized, she could have a much bigger audience than the one packed into contemporary London theaters. Besides, it was an exciting time to be compared to Joan, who was in the process of being canonized, completing a centuries-long process from being vilified as a witch and heretic to reinvention as a saint. In 1869 the French Roman Catholic hierarchy had petitioned the Pope to consider her candidacy for canonization. Then in 1909 she was beatified in Paris at Notre Dame by Pope Pius X, the next step to sainthood, which she achieved almost ten years later. As Millevoye sketched out this seductive new role for Maud, she grasped that the work would engage her in a cause larger than herself, and what's more, she would prove astonishingly successful in the role. Her transformation into the Irish Joan of Arc had begun.

Why did this rich young English woman so empathize with the Irish poor? She behaved as if those evicted by battering ram from their collapsed sod cottages were her parents, siblings, grandparents. Was she as great-hearted as she seemed?

Maud's chosen man was unavailable because he was married. A French divorce was extremely hard to obtain. She knew that Millevoye had a reputation for being a philanderer. This apparently didn't bother her. She didn't need to marry to secure her position in a society that she considered vacuous. Once she turned twenty-one, she had such a vast sum of inherited money that she could be economically independent of any man. She had other choices. Whether or not she wanted to compromise her freedom as a young woman by marriage is doubtful. That Millevoye was married took the possibility off the table, so that may have been another element of his attraction for her. Maud Gonne seemed to have a weakness both for dreamy young poets and for men of action like her father. That could have added to Millevoye's allure for the convalescent young woman. Before the widespread use of antibiotics in the twentieth century, diseases for which there were then no known cures decimated America and Europe. It is intriguing that Maud and Lucien originally met because of their mutual ill health, but both lived a relatively long time. He died at sixty-eight in 1918, she lived another forty-five years, passing away at eighty-seven in 1953.

Maud could have had her pick of men. She attracted a number of admirers in Europe, Ireland, the US, and even in Russia. It is fascinating that she chose a man who was married, with a son. They had to be discreet because of the possibility of a scandal. For more than a decade, Lucien was the most important man in her life. There were others, one of whom, a young poet, proved as significant as Millevoye. For years, she was torn between these two men: the politician and the poet. Divorce in Catholic France was rare. She must have known going into this affair that her chances of marrying her French lover were slim.

At the beginning, Maud's affair with Millevoye must have seemed thrilling, much like her father's youthful commitment to the mighty British imperial forces must have seemed, before he saw the havoc the British army wreaked on populations in near and far parts

of the world. Though no letters between Maud and Lucien ever sur-
faced, their romance, in the age before the invention of the telephone,
must have been fueled by letter writing. The formation of a relationship with someone she couldn't live with was not surprising, given
her upbringing. Her father was never around for extended periods
of time. He would swoop in on weekends when the girls were small,
or on holidays when he was stationed abroad. So, an on-again, off-
again relationship punctuated by travel and absence is what Maud
experienced as a child and as a young woman because of her fond
relationship with her adored but often absent father.

I understood the dynamic of an absent glamorous, adored parent because my own mother, very beautiful and fun to play with and
show off, was not my main caregiver. A governess, then a paid house-
keeper woke me up, took me to school, fed me and my sisters, and
put me to bed at night and heard my prayers. My oldest sister said she
never remembered our mother reading to us. I said, "That's because
she didn't." Nights my mother and my father were home and not
going out were special; we ate together in the formal dining room.
My mother was charming and lively but cold. I didn't experience
much daily affection from either of my parents. My father, sixteen
years older than my mother, was generationally removed from the
crop of current New York fathers, who engage with their children in
a much more meaningful way. To me, as well as to Maud, the unavail-
ability of a lover seemed a tantalizing lure, rather than a deterrent.

After meeting in Royat, Maud and Lucien rendezvoused in the
ancient French port city of Marseilles, where they had a six-day
tryst. No chaperone was in attendance. Lucien gave Maud a small
ivory-handled revolver, an unusual present for a Frenchman to give
his lover, but then she was an unusual woman. He knew she was
sailing on to Constantinople alone. According to one of the many
fabulous tales in Maud's memoir, during a two-hour port stop, she
paid a Greek man with a little rowboat to take her ashore as she badly
wanted to walk on land. After a few hours, she found her oarsman

with some friends and asked him to take her back to her ship, which was moored in their harbor. Instead, she noticed the men were taking her in the opposite direction. Only after she stood up and pointed the revolver at her would-be-kidnapper and said, "Obey or I fire," did he turn the boat around. She was safely returned to her vessel where the captain told her, "None of these ports are safe for a woman alone."

On her way to Turkey, Maud traveled with a pet marmoset, bought in Marseilles with Lucien, and named "Chaperone" in a nod to her own flaunting of social mores. Her father had admonished her as a little girl "to be gay" in letters. An orphan at twenty, she remembered his advice as a young woman and always put up a brave, gay front to the world, which is communicated in her autobiography. The young heiress lacked an actual chaperone during her visit to the home of Sir William White, British ambassador to Turkey, in Constantinople. She and Lila, the ambassador's daughter, were childhood friends and gallivanted around accompanied by a uniformed guard. They amused themselves by dressing up as Turkish princesses and wandering around the embassy's walled garden. Then rumors swirled that the proper White was keeping a harem just like the Sultan who, as the British would call him, was "an infidel." Scandalized, Ambassador White put an end to the girls' theatrics. Maud returned to Europe.

When Maud was back in Paris with her lover, her assignment, as articulated by Lucien, was to forge a Franco–Russian alliance against England. He asked her to deliver papers to the czar's advisor on behalf of his leader, General Boulanger. The letters suggested the czar and the general, a would-be Bonaparte, could make common cause against Germany and become a mighty foil for England. Although scarcely twenty-one, Maud was involved in Lucien's scheme to bring down the British Empire, a huge, daunting undertaking. Not for Maud. To accomplish her mission, Maud took a train to St. Petersburg, a long eventful trip for a young woman with money to see the world in style. On the train, she could marvel at the taste of black caviar and warm her hands on the steaming samovars served to upper-class passengers. When I first saw St. Petersburg's Winter Palace on the edge of the Neva river as a girl, it looked like an image from Coleridge's famous poem "Kubla Khan." Maud too, must have marveled at the Russian baroque architecture of the palace, so different from those of London and Paris. The turquoise blue Winter Palace with its gleaming onion-shaped domes of gold is even grander, more ornate, and gilded inside. The Winter Palace was open to Maud as an upper-class Englishwoman with ties to Russian and French aristocrats, which she had through Millevoye. She duly turned the secret letter over to the Czar Alexander III's advisor, Konstantin Pobedonostsev. However, despite Maud's claim to the contrary, her mission failed. Part of the reason why Boulanger never emerged as a popular, dynamic leader with staying power stemmed from his irresolute character. On crucial occasions he backed down, as he did on this occasion, refusing to verify that Millevoye's message originated with him. So, no one in Russia took the secret letter from Millevoye seriously. Despite the wishes of ardent *boulangistes,* as they were called, the parliamentary system of the Third Republic of France, which they were conspiring to overthrow and return to one-man rule, remained in place from 1870 until 1940, when France was invaded by the Nazis.

Her first espionage trip allowed Maud to playact, which she obviously enjoyed, remembering in her memoir how the secret documents were sewn inside her dark, bouffant traveling skirt. According to her memoir, "I, without a passport, carried to Russia the draft of a treaty, which a few years later, was to change the whole of European diplomacy and alliances in an opposite direction from that desired by England."

It is true Russia's alliances shifted, but not because of General Boulanger or Maud Gonne. World War I and the Russian Revolution intervened. Maud had a talent, as demonstrated in her memoir, for rearranging events for public display, as if she were the heroine of her own splendid adventure story. She was a great mythmaker.

Maud did make her mark in the world, but not as a French spy plotting with Russia to overthrow the French Republic. Instead, the beautiful young Irish nationalist with the compelling voice, the vision, and the money to travel back and forth between Dublin, London, and Paris, the same cities she had frequented as a debutante under her father's watchful eye, made a favorable impression on many, making them aware of the injustices Ireland suffered under the thumb of British Empire. She was eloquent on the need for the formation of an independent Irish Republic. Ambitious and financially independent, she was able to go wherever she pleased and act on her passionate political commitment to Ireland. Her Uncle William could no longer hold her back.

Her longing for a larger purpose was satisfied by the yawning need of Mother Ireland.

She wrote, "I think life without a cause to work for would be very dull and meaningless." She felt the need to stay busy. In 1900, when Yeats's mother died, she counseled work as a tonic for the poet's newly widowed father: "There is nothing like work when one is unhappy." Work was her drug of choice.

By 1890 she became part of a key group of Irish nationalists who spoke up for the evicted and promoted the development of Irish literature, culture, and independence. From the 1880s right up until the establishment of a Republic in 1922, Irishmen had little economic or political power, few local outlets for their frustrations and dreams apart from the church and the pub. Agricultural laborers were paid in their local gathering place: the pub. Not surprisingly, many men spent their money on drink. Slowly in the late nineteenth century, as laws changed, enfranchising more and more Irishmen, so did these stark realities. Another step forward for Ireland was the national schools system created by Britain in 1831, which legalized primary school education in Ireland. The numbers of national schools doubled between 1850 and 1911. Illiteracy decreased radically. Those who could read and write jumped from 33 to 84 percent of the population in the same period.

It is a truism that oppressed people turn to the arts to express their unfulfilled longings. As the writings of Jonathan Swift, Laurence Sterne, Oscar Wilde, and George Bernard Shaw and a seemingly endless list testifies, Irish literature, despite or perhaps because of the Irish history of economic desolation, is extraordinarily rich. To give one example, in 1729 Jonathan Swift wrote and published *A Modest Proposal*, a free pamphlet that satirically addressed the issue of "preventing the children of poor people in Ireland being a burthen to their parents or country, and for making them beneficial to the publick." He sarcastically suggested that parents sell plump babies of a year old for consumption at "the table." Irish writers like Swift relied on their wit and way with words because they had no other weapons at their disposal. They were governed by the hostile, self-serving rule of British law.

A century and a half after the circulation of *A Modest Proposal*, Maud Gonne became an ardent modern voice for Irish men and women who responded enthusiastically to her words and to her appealing person. After her father's death, Maud returned to Dublin and began what proved to be her life's work. At first, she stayed with her childhood friend Ida Jameson, of the wealthy distillery-owning Jameson family, in the suburb of Donnybrook. As in London, and the Trafalgar Square protests, Maud quickly found other important Irish nationalists in Dublin, a much smaller city where everyone seemed to know each other. Ida introduced her to Charles Hubert Oldham, a Home Rule supporter and Trinity College mathematics professor who was editor and cofounder of the *Dublin University Review*. He published the first poems of W. B. Yeats and the writings of Douglas Hyde, the Irish nationalist, scholar, and diplomat who became the first president of the republic in 1938. Yeats toiled for years as a very public, Irish-centric poet before winning the Nobel Prize for

Literature in 1923. As a young woman in her early twenties, Maud moved in circles with the men who became the leading Irish nationalists, writers, and intellectuals of their time.

At the invitation of Charles Oldham, Maud began to attend meetings of the Contemporary Club, which he had founded. A club like many other Dublin societies where debates continued throughout the night, members discussed the hot button issues of the day, including politics and literature, and they were entirely male. Women weren't permitted to join men's nationalist or literary societies—or to vote—but they were allowed into the Contemporary Club as guests of male members. Maud Gonne, with her beauty, stature, and enthusiasm made quite an impression on the members, including the venerated Irish nationalist leader John O'Leary. Under the British Treason Felony Law, O'Leary had been convicted of conspiring with other Fenians, members of a secret brotherhood whose name meant "brave warrior" in Irish. These Irishmen known as "Fenians" in Ireland and America were plotting how best to overthrow their English colonial rulers and establish an independent Irish republic. O'Leary paid for his beliefs with twenty years of imprisonment and exile. In 1885, he finally returned to Dublin at fifty-nine. O'Leary, with his leonine head and great white beard, cut an imposing figure; despite his relatively young age, he looked like an extremely old man.

By then O'Leary believed that there was no fine literature in the world without nationality, an idea that influenced the young Yeats. O'Leary thought Ireland had to have a cultural revolution before it could have a national one. He and others believed the Irish had to throw off the superficial mask of English culture, reveal Irish folklore and long-forgotten myths underneath, then use both to fashion a new unique Irish culture. As Yeats brilliantly demonstrated, the Irish could use old myths to develop a modern cosmopolitan literature of their own, separate from England's. As with many other important ideas, this was discussed at the Contemporary Club and the National Literary Society, another organization, founded by W. B.

Yeats. Douglas Hye, another up-and-coming figure in the nationalist movement, was the president.

In Dublin, Maud experienced the heady power of being a beautiful woman who could command attention just by walking into a roomful of men. Men would stop what they were doing to look at her, and try to be of assistance. Conscious of her looks, Maud exploited them for effect. Young Maud befriended John O'Leary, one of her many admirers. When she humbly asked how to become better acquainted with the Fenian movement, he advised her to read, suggested books, and allowed her to use his house in Rathmines, Dublin as her library.

The tart-tongued O'Leary became her champion until a decade later, when she crossed a line he would not follow. Disparaging his own initial favorable response to Maud, he complained to Yeats, "She is no disciple of mine. . . . she went there [to Tipperary] to show off her new bonnets." He didn't approve of Maud's getting involved with the Nationalist League and agrarian reform, probably because he himself owned and rented out land. The Jameson parents also disapproved of Maud's nationalist activities; they were Unionists in favor of Ireland remaining part of Great Britain.

With her financial resources, Maud was fortunately able to leave the Jameson home for Dublin's elegant Gresham Hotel, still one of the finest hotels in that vibrant city. At the Gresham she met Douglas Hyde, then a collector of traditional Irish folklore and a budding politician. He attempted to teach her Irish, but she traveled too much to successfully undertake the challenge of learning a new language and gave up in a few months. By then Hyde had become another admirer. On December 16, 1888, he confided to his diary, "I saw the most dazzling woman I have ever seen: Miss Gonne who drew every male gaze in the room around her. . . . We stayed talking until 1:30 AM. My head was spinning with her beauty."

Her response to Hyde was prosaic. In her memoir, she listed him among the many new friends she made in Dublin: James Connolly,

Arthur Griffith, and Willie Rooney, all became important names in the Irish nationalist movement. After moving out of the Gresham Hotel and taking rooms in Nassau Street above a popular bookstore and library, Maud wrote of her lively new acquaintances: "Many took the habit of dropping in to see me when the Library closed, for we all kept late hours in Dublin in those days, and went home with the milk." Then as now Dublin had a reputation for being a city of talkers, meaning people who loved the art of conversation.

In some areas, such as learning Irish, Maud was a dilettante who dabbled. In others, she plunged right in and stuck it out. If one avenue didn't work, she just tried another. For example, in her early days as an independent adult in Dublin, she tried to meet Charles Stewart Parnell. Known as "Ireland's uncrowned king," Parnell was leader of the parliamentary movement known as Home Rule, which would have given Ireland its own Parliament, separate from England's. He refused to meet with Maud. He didn't take women nationalists seriously. For political reasons, he withdrew support for his sister Anna Parnell's Ladies' Land League and forced its dissolution. Finally, a few years later in 1891, Maud had dinner with Parnell and his doctor, who was a mutual friend. She had attained her goal.

Regardless of her sex, Maud was able to become part of the campaign. We don't know what Maud's conservative British uncle William thought of his niece becoming an Irish nationalist. Perhaps they cut ties once she achieved notoriety in the papers. Perhaps they never saw one another again after Kathleen Gonne's 1891 London wedding. Since Maud never mentions him again in either letters or her memoir, this seems likely.

Like a stone dropped in a lake sending out ripples, after first introductions Maud had a widening circle of Dublin contacts. Her desire was for action more than study, though she was clearly very intelligent. Of herself then she wrote: "Being young and hasty, I secretly felt action not books was needed; I did not then realize how the written word may lead to action and I drifted off to speak at other meetings held on wild hillsides, where resistance to evictions was being organized."

Poor Millevoye: when he invited her to be the Irish Joan of Arc he had no idea that she would take it so seriously that Ireland would become her second home. In Dublin, Maud met the Irish MP, nationalist politician, journalist, and lawyer Timothy Harrington. He was secretary for the Irish National League, which aimed to reform rental laws in Ireland. Once again, because she was a woman, Maud could not join.

However, Harrington assessed her correctly and realized she had money and passion to spare. He asked if she would investigate and publicize the conditions of the evicted in northwest County Donegal. Eviction and land reform were to become key issues in the evolution of Ireland from a Third World backwater to a prosperous republic. Harrington's request appealed to Maud because she wanted to take action to help the Irish poor she had seen from a distance as a debutante. To perform her assignment, Harrington introduced her to field organizers and the so-called "fighting priests." They supported collective bargaining by tenant farmers to reduce high rents. Once again, after an agricultural depression, thousands had been evicted.

One of Donegal's local fighting priests, Father James McFadden, had a reputation for standing in the doorways of tenants' dirt-floor hovels and barring the way to policemen. On February 3, 1889, when the Royal Irish Constabulary tried to arrest McFadden, the irate crowd killed one of the RIC. Going to Donegal and standing up for tenant's rights was dangerous work. Maud, the brave captain's daughter, did not seem frightened at the prospect of violence, either by police or by the mob. Did she like the excitement of seeking out hot spots? Perhaps for the grown woman, as for the child, it was an exercise in bravery and proving how like her father she was. Maud loved operatic drama and knew how to make an entrance calculated for maximum impact.

On this adventure, she traveled west to Donegal with her Great Dane, Dagda, named after the Celtic deity associated with

wisdom and magic. She invited her adventurous cousin May, by then
a trained nurse, and also brought a groom for the horses. What the
two genteel women saw horrified them: large tenant families including grandparents, infants, and mothers recovering from childbirth
were evicted from their homes with battering rams by the police.
The full apparatus of British law wrecked the cottages and put people
who couldn't pay their rent out to live on the side of the road.

In 1891, over several trips to the small towns of Gweedore and to
Falcarragh in Donegal, Maud helped evicted families build new huts
of stone and thatch. Otherwise their alternatives were bleak: dying
of exposure in the cold and the rain or being separated by sex and age
at the poorhouse. Maud herself stayed in small hotel rooms, where
she gave shelter to the most desperate of the evicted. She also organized soup kitchens and attended the trials of children being fined and
sent to prison because they had "stolen" turf for fire and seaweed to
heat their homes. The children had stolen from the eighteen-thou-
sand-acre estate of Colonel Wybrants Olphert, one of a number of
landlords adamantly refusing the pleas of both priests and tenant
farmers to lower rents when harvests were bad. Instead, he evicted a
thousand people from their homes because they could not pay their
rent. The displaced went to the poorhouse, died of exposure, or were
forced to emigrate. Choices were few.

Maud began to see firsthand the truth of how the majority of
Irish lived. In a statement to the Bureau of Military History, Maud
said her first up-close view of evictions reminded her of when she
lost her mother, when she was four, and heard a kind woman who
took her and her sister and their nurse in out of the rain, say: "The
creatures, God help them, they have lost their mother." Witnessing
people losing their home reminded Maud of her childhood loss. She
empathized with the families she was helping because she linked
their misfortune with her own.

Country people began to call young Maud "the Woman
of the Sidhe," meaning woman of the fairy people. Dressed in

Paris-made outfits, close to six feet tall, riding on a horse through the countryside, followed by her faithful Great Dane, Maud must have cut a striking figure, particularly to the impoverished rural Irish. "They are saying you are a woman of the Sidhe who rode into Donegal on a white horse surrounded by birds to bring victory," said Father McFadden. Also according to Maud, the legend surrounding her grew. She certainly dressed for affect and at the same time she actually played the part of a bounteous beauty from one of French writer Charles Perrault's fairytales, but a very practical fairy who organized soup kitchens for the hungry evicted tenants. She seemed too good to be true.

In Donegal, she had further opportunity to express her values in dramatic Maud-like fashion. When an admiring old liberal MP followed her down from London into the wild Irish countryside, he presented her with a diamond pendant and asked her to be his wife. Maud, according to her memoir, handed the pendant to the woman of the house and said the kind gentleman wished her to sell the pendant and use the money to feed her family. The furious MP, tactfully called "Sir John" by Maud, left in a huff. Then he came back and bought the pendant for the sum owed for rent. There is no way to verify this anecdote as the source is Maud, whom we know was a good storyteller but an unreliable narrator.

As if that weren't drama enough, Lucien Millevoye wanted to know what was keeping Maud from him and their first child, Georges Ernest Silvere, named after Millevoye's hero. The baby was born on August 11, 1890. The child had been conceived in the dark days for the Boulangists when the movement collapsed. Maud must have consoled her devastated lover in ways that lovers have done for centuries because their child was born nine months later. So it may have been for the sake of his son, as well as himself, that Lucien Millevoye pursued Maud to Ireland. He couldn't understand why she was spending so long away from him and their life together in Paris. Maud had no idea he was in Ireland too until she got a pleading letter from him sent from Donegal. He was nearby, but sick. He didn't speak English well, according to Maud, so he really needed her. If Millevoye wasn't healthy, as his frequent spa sojourns suggest, he must have admired Maud's strength, her will, and her determination. He may have wished to reserve her strong fund of energy for himself and their child rather than see it "wasted" on the Irish. To some extent, Millevoye's efforts worked. Upon receipt of his letter, Maud immediately went to him. She found his "hand hot with fever" and spent a week nursing him back to health. Then she sent him on his way to Paris without her. The two lovers quarreled first. Millevoye only wanted Maud to work for Ireland from Paris, not spend months at a time away from him in that impoverished island. Lucien, a right-wing politician, a conservative, thought that like more conventional mothers, she should be with their baby boy. When Maud was out of town, Georges lived with his caregiver in Samois-sur-Seine, near the forest of Fontainebleau, a brief train ride from Paris. When Maud was in Paris, they were "ensemble" in her apartment. Maud, who had been raised by a nurse herself, seemed to have no problem leaving her baby behind while she was working for Ireland.

In Dublin, after her trip to Donegal, Maud reported back to Harrington. He was impressed by her first-person accounts and suggested she come with him to England to campaign for a Liberal Party candidate, James Archibald Duncan, who was in favor of Home Rule. A political star was born. Harrington wanted ordinary English people to hear her speak about the dreadful poverty in the west of Ireland. She did as he asked. Prepped by Harrington, fifteen hundred people turned out for her first speech in Lancashire, England. Describing the desolation she had seen in Donegal, Maud burst into tears and sat down, face in her handkerchief, sobbing. The audience stood and applauded.

After the hurdle of her first solo speech, Maud found she could address large meetings without stage fright. She already knew she could campaign door to door. Duncan, the candidate she had canvassed for, won. Maud's notoriety was growing. She earned her first Dublin police report in August 1890. Now, after her electioneering work in Britain, her picture was posted in the British society pages over photographs taken of her as a debutante a few years before.

On the crest of her notoriety, Maud made use of John and Ellen O'Leary's introductions to visit the extraordinarily talented Yeats family, then living in Bedford Park, London on January 30, 1889. O'Leary knew John Butler Yeats as a distinguished Irish portrait painter. Yeats had done a painting of John O'Leary which now hangs in the National Portrait Gallery, Dublin. The two families, both ardently nationalist, became friends, and it was during sittings for his portrait that John O'Leary first heard the young Willie read his poetry. Impressed, he told the young Yeats that he should be a poet, like his sister Ellen O'Leary, who had recommended the senior Yeats meet Maud because of their overlapping interests.

The Yeats family faced multiple hardships. Like her husband, John Butler Yeats, Susan Pollexfen was of Irish Protestant middle-class stock. Her family was quite prosperous. However, affluence couldn't protect the Pollefexens from the familial strain of mental instability. That dark thread became evident as the Pollexfen children grew up. One of Susan's sisters was confined intermittently to an asylum, and her brother died in one. Susan faced many challenges and it sounds as if her mental health, like that of her siblings, was compromised, and exacerbated by the harsh realities of her life. Soon after marriage, Susan Yeats had seven children in quick succession; two died as toddlers, which left her heartbroken and understandably depressed. As if that weren't enough to make a young mother despair, her husband gave up the law after a few years and, at age twenty-eight, decided to go to art school in London. As Susan feared, the family struggled financially for the rest of their lives, though her children eventually climbed out of penury. Their father was a talented painter but never made a living from his art. Instead, he lived off his wife's rich family, later rich friends and acquaintances, and then later still off the meager income of his four children. As his Pollexfen in-laws discovered, John Butler Yeats did not repay his debts.

Yeats's mother lived until the poet was thirty-five. Unlike her children and husband, who were prolific journal and letter writers, Susan Yeats left behind no written account with her side of the family story. Her response to their impoverished life was to retreat inward. She absented herself from the constant worries about the family's finances. When Yeats was a teenager and later a young man, his mother couldn't be a steady source of affection or intellectual stimulation for him or his siblings. As an adult, Yeats felt pity for her. For him, as for Maud, there was a gaping hole in his family life; unlike Maud, his own mother was alive, but often sadly unavailable.

During the summers, the Yeats children were left with their loving grandparents, aunts, and uncles in a fourteen-bedroom mansion in Sligo, Ireland. From ages five to nine, William Butler Yeats and his three siblings lived with their grandparents. In 1881, when Willie was a teen, his father moved the entire family to Howth, the same seaside village on the bay where Maud and her sister spent their childhood. Money was such an issue that when Willie took the train to Dublin in high school, he would go meet his father at his painting studio for his next two meals. In his father's studio, young Willie had tea with plain bread and butter for both his breakfast and his lunch.

By 1888, the Yeats family had regrouped and gathered to live together in an attractive but cheap house in Bedford Park, London. By then, Susan Pollexfen Yeats had suffered two strokes. She was forty-seven years old, and would spend most of her next twelve remaining years in an upstairs bedroom. In contrast, the Yeats children were beginning to make their way in the world as artists. Jack, like his father, was a painter (and years later was praised by no less a critic than fellow Irishman Samuel Beckett). William was a budding poet, writer, editor, and critic. Lolly took up teaching art to children, while Lily, who worked in embroidery, was the only one of the five who brought in a regular salary. "We were always paupers," Lily remembered. Sometimes the children, now young adults, went hungry.

The Yeats family's new neighbors in Bedford Park were journalists, artists, academics, poets, playwrights, even an anarchist, drawn by the low rents. The windy, tree-lined streets were considered unfashionable. It wasn't one of the better London neighborhoods but it was affordable for the Yeats family, and the canny John Butler Yeats negotiated the price of the house down for his family of six. This was the slightly shabby townhouse, with its garden of brilliant yellow sunflowers and foxtail amaranth, a blossom resembling fuchsia-colored drooping tassels, where the family lived when the twenty-three-year-old Maud arrived in a hansom cab in January 1889. Since it was winter, the garden must have looked stark to Maud when she arrived, with nothing in bloom, but it was the inhabitants inside the house that she was interested in, not the garden.

All her life Maud had admired artists, always keeping *au courant*, and she hoped to add John Butler Yeats's family to her widening circle of nationalist friends, acquaintances, and admirers. She rode from Belgravia to the Yeats's western London suburb and kept the cab waiting during her visit. The high cost of keeping a cab impressed Lolly as an extravagance that she duly noted in her diary. Lolly summed Maud up: "She is immensely tall and very stylish and well-dressed in a careless way." Her unimpressed sister Lily observed their visitor wore slippers rather than proper shoes. W. B. Yeats's reaction was cataclysmic. The poet remembered:

> I was twenty-three years old when the troubling of my life began. As I look backward, it seems to me that she brought into my life—for as yet I saw only what lay upon the surface—the middle of a tint, a sound as of a Burmese gong, an overpowering tumult that had yet many pleasant secondary notes.

I had never thought to see in a living woman so great a beauty. It belonged to famous pictures, to poetry, to some legendary past. A complexion like the blossom of apples through which the light falls by a great heap of such blossoms in the window . . . and a stature so great that she seemed of a divine race.

The meeting of these two was profound. Yeats's obsession with Maud arguably lasted to the end of his life, when she figured in one of his final poems. Their complicated relationship simmered, bubbled, flamed high, then low for forty-five years. It bridged the Victorian and modern eras and arguably helped usher in the first independent Irish republic in five hundred years. How it played out in both their lives is a far-fetched tale of love and obsession.

Within a few weeks of their meeting, Yeats wrote to Ellen O'Leary, "Did I tell you how much I admire Miss Gonne? If she said the world was flat or the moon an old caubeen [an Irish beret] tossed up in the sky I would be proud to be of her party." He fell, and fell hard, but no matter how much Yeats admired Maud Gonne, at twenty-three he was in no position to marry a beautiful woman. He had no money, nor expectations of inheriting any. As Yeats wrote in his memoir, "What wife could she make. I thought, what share could she have in the life of a student?" Young Yeats spent much time studying the occult, poetry, and theater. Industrious and ambitious, he was editing an edition of Blake's poems, working on a collection of Irish folktales, and writing the play *Cathleen ni Houlihan* and a volume of his own poems. All this labor added up to a pittance that left him unable to move from the family's rented home in Bedford Park.

In the spring of 1889, the Boulanger movement imploded. The rumor that the French government was going to put out a warrant for the general's arrest for treason triggered Boulanger's flight from Paris. Rather than leading an insurrection, the general and his mistress Madame de Bonnemains abandoned their supporters and their dream and fled to Belgium by train. Perhaps to console her crushed lover, Maud returned to Paris where she rented an apartment on 66 Avenue de Wagram and conceived their first child.

Though pregnant, Maud managed to travel to London. When her sister Kathleen fell ill, improved, and then relapsed, Maud came several times to nurse her back to health. She looked after those, like her beloved nurse, lucky enough to be within her close family circle. The fragility of her own health didn't stop her. In December 1889, Kathleen married Thomas David Pilcher, a British army officer like their father. Pregnant, Maud went to London for the wedding. It is hard to imagine how Maud hid her final trimester of pregnancy from her stuffy Uncle William, who would have been present at the wedding of his niece and former ward. But Maud, ever a master of costuming, evidently managed to do so.

Maud kept her life in Paris with her married French lover and their baby boy a secret from her uncle as well as most others, including Yeats. In 1890, being an unwed mother in either devoutly Catholic, increasingly nationalist, revolutionary Ireland or in Victorian England was scandalous. The mother and child would have been shunned or turned out on the streets. It was a dangerous game that Maud was playing. Luckily, she had enough money to pay for a household for the baby and his nurse. In Maud's little house, she and Lucien could meet. In the sophisticated world of nineteenth-century Paris, such arrangements occurred, but discreetly.

Maud admitted she was the child's mother only to her sister and her cousins May and Chotie. Possibly to tamp down Yeats's ardor, in the summer of 1891 she wrote to him that she'd had a dream that in a past life they were a brother and sister sold into slavery in the Arabian Desert. Far from cooling Yeats's passion, the dream inspired him to travel across the Irish Sea to Dublin from London to propose. Maud turned him down, stating there were reasons that she could not marry. Like, for example, her child with Millevoye, but she did not share that information with him.

Sexually frustrated but still ardent, Yeats kept in close touch. In his memoir he records they saw each other daily. They visited Howth, the landscape of both their childhoods, walked the cliffs they loved, and watched the seagulls wheeling out over the sea. The seagull was Maud's favorite bird. Based on this experience, Yeats wrote a series of love poems that he sent to Maud, including "The White Birds" (1892):

> I would that we were, my beloved, white birds on the foam of the sea!
>
> ....
>
> For I would we were changed to white birds on the wandering foam: I and you!
>
> I am haunted by numberless islands and many a Danaan shore,
>
> Where Time would surely forget us, and Sorrow come near us no more.

Danaan refers to a supernatural race in Celtic mythology. Interrupting their lovely time together that August, Maud received a telegram from Lucien that their son was very ill. She abruptly told Yeats she needed to return to Paris, inventing an excuse.

Nothing could be done to save little Georges, who had contracted meningitis, in the pre-antibiotic era. He died a few weeks later on August 31, 1891, aged eighteen months. She wrote Yeats a letter of "wild sorrow" about the death of a child she had adopted. The new mother was distraught. She became addicted to chloroform, forgot the French she had learned as a child; her mood became as black as her mourning clothes. Millevoye would eventually help shame her into giving up the anesthetic. According to Maud, her cousin May, a nurse, came to stay with her and would hide the bottle. But Maud always found it, even when it was hidden under ashes in the maid's fireplace.

> I was so proud of this exhibition of uncanny knowledge that I boasted of it next day at lunch. Millevoye was lunching with us. "Yes," he said sarcastically, "it is just as wonderful as a drunkard in a strange place can always find the pub." I was very angry, but the thought remained. After all, it was just the same force, some evil spirit perhaps guiding me. I went into my room and took the bottle and broke it and after that fought insomnia without drugs. I refused to let any will, human or disincarnate, overpower my own. I was not quite certain I had won that battle till I got another bottle and was able to leave it untouched by my bed.

As with so many other incidents in her life, Maud gives no date for her battle with chloroform. It is significant because Millevoye played a positive role, and it also ties into Maud's belief that no one in the world could overpower her will.

After Georges's death, Maud spent 10,000 francs (roughly equivalent to $47,000 in 2019) to embalm her little boy's body in a large white marble tomb in the Samois cemetery. Lucien must have been doubly distraught because the death of his baby boy in August was followed by the distressing news one month later of General Boulanger's suicide. In Brussels, the general shot himself on his mistress's grave. She had died three months earlier, and the romantic indecisive soldier couldn't live without her.

On October 11 Maud returned to Dublin on the same boat that carried Charles Stewart Parnell's body home for burial. She was dressed entirely in black and many naturally assumed she was mourning the tragic death of Parnell. After he'd been named and sued in divorce court, Parnell's career in Catholic Ireland was over.

Refusing to give up, but fatigued and sick from campaigning in the soaking cold rain, Parnell died of pneumonia in his new wife's arms. He was forty-five. Contrary to appearances, Maud was not mourning the dashed hopes for Home Rule with Parnell's death. She grieved for her child.

Upon arriving in Dublin, Yeats met her at the quay. He saw her frequently throughout her visit. He wrote: "She had come to have need of me, and I had no doubt that need would become love, that it was already coming so. I had even as I watched her a sense of cruelty, as though I were a hunter taking captive some beautiful wild creature."

But her talks with him that fall weren't of love, or her dead child. Instead they were of their joint quest to contact the otherworld of ancient Irish gods and goddesses. Yeats, already a member of the Order of the Golden Dawn, initiated her into the London based order on November 2, 1891. The study of the occult, metaphysics, magic, and "astral" travel (the term for traveling without one's body) were the givens of this secret, multilevel order, founded by three Freemasons. Freemasons are a secretive international fraternal order. Unlike the Golden Dawn, they accepted no women. The emphasis on rituals and levels of importance within their hierarchies are similar. However, the Golden Dawn emphasized otherworldly phenomena. It was not a religion, though it contained elements of religious thought and also of theosophy, an Eastern-flavored quasi-religion founded in 1875 by the Russian mystic Helena Blavatsky.

Such philosophies were the rage in late nineteenth-century Europe and the United States. Not just poets but scientists believed in the occult. For instance, the Nobel Prize-winning chemists Marie and Pierre Curie participated in séances. Later, a grief-stricken Marie would attempt to communicate with her dead husband.

For Yeats, such otherworldly beliefs were among the useful waystations through which he traveled intellectually in order to build the intricate structure of what he came to call his "vision." As a young man, before he published *A Vision* in 1925, his membership in the Golden Dawn and cultivation of "magic" helped shape his increasingly powerful poetry. Unlike Yeats, Maud didn't stay in the Order of the Golden Dawn for many years, yet she shared some of their otherworld and cyclical belief of history. She participated in many séances with Yeats and his friends.

On October 20, before she left Dublin, Yeats gave Maud *The Flame of the Spirit*, a white calfskin notebook inscribed with her name, containing a haunting set of poems, including "Cycles Ago," in which the poet riffs on her dream of their being brother and sister "before this life had begun." Then he wrote an early draft of another poem to Maud called "When You Are Old." It is one of the more gorgeous lyrics of twentieth-century poetry:

When you are old and grey and full of sleep,
And nodding by the fire, take down this book,
And slowly read, and dream of the soft look
Your eyes had once, and of their shadows deep;

How many loved your moments of glad grace,
And loved your beauty with love false or true,
But one man loved the pilgrim soul in you,
And loved the sorrows of your changing face

When Maud went back to Paris, her cousin May, her confidante from childhood, advised Yeats to follow. But Yeats was broke. He had to borrow a pound from O'Leary to pay for his share of cabs when she returned to London that winter. He didn't like her to pay for him and always insisted on paying his share. It is notable that though in the early years of their friendship Yeats and Maud shared so much about themselves, including their childhoods and their dreams for the future of Ireland, nowhere is it ever recorded that they discussed their financial differences. Perhaps Yeats was embarrassed to talk about his pressing financial concerns to his adored one. She too may have held back discussing money, other than insisting on paying her own way, because of a certain restraint.

Maud had begun to focus her formidable energy on her lover in Paris. She used her growing familiarity with the occult for intensely personal, private reasons, constructing a unique antidote for grief. Her hope was that her dead child's spirit would live again in a new baby's body. She and Yeats had a friend, the painter, poet, and mystic George William Russell, known by the pseudonym AE, who told Maud that the spirit of a dead child could be reborn to the same parents under certain circumstances. In séances with the young seer AE and Yeats, she explored otherworldly possibilities of life after death. When she returned to Paris, Maud clung to AE's idea. In Samois-sur-Seine in the white marble mausoleum she built to hold the embalmed body of her baby boy, Maud convinced Lucien, her estranged lover, to have sex. Her hope was that her dead child's spirit could live again in a new baby's body. Though Yeats may have intuited that Maud's "adopted boy" was more to her than that, he knew neither of her new plan nor its successful execution until much, much later. Like Maud, Yeats believed in mythology mixed with otherworldly, supernatural elements. Both Yeats and Gonne were susceptible to the current beliefs in the occult.

Sisters Kathleen and Maud Gonne (Maud at right),
Maud Gonne Collection, Emory University.

A teenaged Maud Gonne in Paris, Maud Gonne Collection, Emory University.

Maud as a debutante, circa 1886, National Library of Ireland.

Countess de la Sizeranne, Maud's great aunt, in Florence, n.d. Maud Gonne Collection, Stuart A. Rose Manuscript, Archives and Rare Book Library, Emory University.

A vintage travel poster depicting Royat, the French spa the Gonne women visited in 1886. Courtesy of the author.

Lucien Millevoye, courtesy of Iseult White.

Maud with her beloved Dagda, 1889, courtesy of Iseult White.

*William Butler Yeats at 3 Blenheim Road, Bedford Park,
circa 1890.*

Maud in Boston during her second US tour. She wears her favorite Tara brooch,
a Celtic symbol with medieval origins. James Purdy, circa 1900,
National Library of Ireland.

Chapter 4
A Not-So-Immaculate Conception: Single Motherhood in Belle Époque Paris

Maud made as big a splash in Paris as she had among the group of Irish nationalist men in Dublin. Why did she use Paris as a home base for almost thirty years (1890–1918) during the Belle Époque, instead of Dublin or London? The answer is simple. It was safer for an unwed mother than the other cities, where the disapproving censure of society would have been crippling. No one would have come to Maud's late-night politicking sessions in her apartment above a bookstore in Dublin if they knew she had a child out of wedlock. She would have been labeled a "wicked, immoral woman." In contemporary London, as in Dublin, she would have been shunned.

Instead, in Paris she rented apartments on beautiful wide boulevards—at 66 Avenue de la Grande Armée, then at 7 Avenue d'Eylau, both within sight of the just completed Eiffel Tower. She traveled between Paris, London, Dublin, and the Irish countryside and folded in three lecture tours of the United States. After her voyages by train, boat, and horseback when she was young, Paris was the place to which she returned. Her children were born there, where they were raised by friends, relatives, caregivers, and Maud.

Paris during the Belle Époque was an amazing place to live. The period lasted from 1871, the end of the Franco–Prussian War, to the start of the First World War in 1914. During those forty-three years of peace, the artistic life of the city flowered. Henri Matisse, Pierre-Auguste Renoir, Camille Pissarro, Claude Debussy, Erik Satie,

Sarah Bernhardt, and Marcel Proust lived in Paris. Much of Proust's enduring masterpiece À la recherche du temps perdu (In Search of Lost Time) was written during the Belle Époque in Paris. Married in 1895, the brilliant scientists Marie and Pierre Curie, who together discovered radioactivity, labored, loved, lived, and died in Paris. The radical politician Georges Clemenceau also lived there, where he went from being mayor of the city to prime minister of the entire country. Colette, the sensuous, bisexual writer and performer who made Maud's clandestine life look positively sedate, was another luminary who lived in Paris from 1893 (apart from a few years spent touring in music halls with her cross-dressing partner Mathilde de Morny, known as "Missy") until her death in 1954, a year after Maud.

La Belle Époque was a period of immense population growth and eye-catching new construction. The iron latticework of the Eiffel Tower; the Paris Métro, the city's underground lifeline; and the Paris Opera, one of the loveliest opera houses in all of Europe were built and finished during the period. When it was completed in 1889, the Eiffel Tower was the tallest manmade structure in the world. It had been engineered, designed, and built entirely by Frenchmen. Millions came to visit the beautiful city of Paris with its many cheerful window boxes and glorious flower markets during the World's Fairs of 1889 and 1900. In thirty years, the population of Paris almost doubled, reaching 2,888,000 in 1911, half a million higher than it is today.

In 1890–1891, when Maud took her first apartment in Paris, it was the most cosmopolitan of European cities, the most sophisticated, and arguably, the loosest in its morals, as Maud must have realized. For instance, in 1878 the rising political leader and publisher Georges Clemenceau separated from his American wife and found other lady companions. Mornings, Clemenceau could be found riding through the fashionable Bois de Boulogne with his latest dalliance, on the same boulevard where teenaged Maud took carriage rides with her great-aunt Mary. The goal for ambitious politicians and socialites was the same: to see and be seen by the important members of French society. In 1892, after multiple adulteries by him and one by his wife, Clemenceau divorced her. This didn't affect his political career in the slightest. He went on to play many roles in French public life, from mayor of Paris to prime minister of the republic.

Compare this to the career of the Irish MP Charles Stewart Parnell, the "uncrowned king of Ireland." With the assistance of the swing vote of the Irish Nationalist Party, helmed by Parnell, British Prime Minister William Ewart Gladstone tried to pass Home Rule for Ireland in 1886 and again in 1893. The proposed bills would have allowed Ireland its own parliament, and to pass its own laws. While remaining under British sovereignty, Ireland would have been able to govern itself for the first time in five hundred years. Gladstone had adroitly formed an alliance with Parnell though he remained Victorian and Anglican in his own behavior. He thought the best part of life was public life; politics was a "blessed calling" that demanded he apply his "Christian principles."

So in 1889 all hell broke loose in this constricted political landscape when Parnell was named co-respondent in an adultery case by an Irish MP, Captain William O'Shea. The ensuing trial proved that Parnell was not only the lover of O'Shea's wife Kitty, but also the father of three of the married couple's four children. The O'Sheas had separated around 1880, and Parnell and Kitty O'Shea had been living together without the sacrament of marriage ever since. When Captain O'Shea's divorce was granted, Parnell could finally marry her.

However, Parnell's political career was ruined by the revelation of the affair. Methodist and Evangelical members of the Liberal Party and the entire Irish Catholic hierarchy immediately demanded Parnell's resignation. He refused, and the Liberal Party and the Irish Parliamentary Party split into factions for and against Parnell. In 1892, with his glittering political future shattered, Parnell fought for reelection in cold wet Irish weather. He caught pneumonia and died, aged forty-five. Irish nationalist Parnell's comet-like rise and fall could be seen as a cautionary tale to Maud.

Ironically, Maud was following in a family tradition by having a child out of wedlock. In 1897 while she was living in London with Uncle William, a strange young woman rang the doorbell, interrupting their tea. Her name was Margaret Wilson and she confessed she had been Maud's father Tommy Gonne's lover. In 1887, a few months after his death, Margaret had given birth to a girl she named Eileen, and was only reluctantly revealing her "shameful" secret to Tommy's family. She had been too ill to work and needed money to support herself and the child. Upset by the scandal, William Gonne gave her five sovereigns, equivalent now to about $1,000, and ushered her out.

Maud's response was warmer. She remembered her father asking her to write a check to a Margaret Wilson before he died. She hadn't recognized the name. In her late twenties, Margaret was only a few years older than Maud. Taking responsibility for her half-sister, Maud arranged to place baby Eileen with her own nurse, Bowie, who had retired to a cottage outside London. Maud kindly supported the child until the little girl grew up and married, but Maud treated the child's mother Margaret very differently.

In 1892, Maud met Ignatiy Platonovich Zakrevsky, a rich Russian in Dublin. He was looking for an English-speaking governess for his twin girls. Maud persuaded Margaret to take the job, though it was far away on the eastern border of Estonia, closer to Finland and Russia than England. It was a job Margaret, or "Mickey" as the Zakrevsky children called her, would hold for fifty-six years as a beloved family member. It was generous and open-minded of Maud by the standards of Victorian England to help her father's mistress, but Margaret never saw her daughter again. Instead she raised the Zakrevsky children and grandchildren as if they were her own, while the fate of Eileen remained entwined with that of the Gonne family. Perhaps Maud had some latent hostility towards Margaret, the vulnerable young woman who had secured her father's amorous affections during the time she imagined herself as his only female companion. Unlike her father's mistress, Maud would raise her child as a single mother without being cast out from society, because she had the means to do so.

In August 1894, at the age of twenty-eight, Maud gave birth to a daughter, Iseult. She referred to the girl as her niece or adopted daughter. Iseult learned to call her mother Moura, an anagram of *amour*, but never mother. Her second child slowed Maud down during her pregnancy, and for the first year of the new baby's life, but within nine months Maud returned to public view: her name was in the papers again by May 1895. While still in her mid-twenties, Maud had expanded her influence from speaking about Irish politics and being the subject of articles to writing about Irish affairs as a budding journalist. Journalism was a new and powerful force in the politics of the late nineteenth century. Emerging nations, increased literacy, and low costs led to a growing newspaper readership among the masses. Maud began to make a name for herself in this new world of cheap, popular newspapers and magazines. Those newspapers were made possible by the invention of high-speed presses, along with the invention of wood pulp technology. Paper became cheap and fueled mass printing. *United Ireland*, a nationalist newspaper started by a deputy of Parnell's, cost a penny in 1892. Maud intelligently used news media to make her views known to a growing audience in France, England, Ireland, and America.

In 1891, her first published article, "Un Peuple Opprimé" ("An Oppressed People"), appeared in *La Nouvelle Revue Internationale*. Lucien had introduced her to the editor, Marie Bonaparte-Wyse, Napoleon I's great-niece, who was known as a writer and leader of a Paris salon. In the article, Maud described how "Every day the misery [of the evicted in Ireland] spreads like an epidemic." She "was just a witness who cried, and what woman would not shed tears when faced with such suffering?" She reported on the evictions she had witnessed: a 103-year-old man forced from "his miserable hut";

a woman in bed after childbirth, deposited in the mud outside her cottage by the police, her husband legally helpless to stop them from enforcing the law. "Poor little white slaves" she called the seven- and eight-year-old children sent by their impoverished parents north to work for rich farm owners in Ulster. Maud went for the pathos in her first story to win over French readers. She hoped French opinion would influence French politics. Her ultimate goal was for France to once again ally herself with Ireland as during the failed 1798 rebellion when, motivated by their rivalry with the English, French ships and troops crossed the sea to aid the Irish. Maud wished to sway world opinion against the British and raise money in France and in America to fund another Irish rebellion. Her evocative language worked for both her editors and her readers. She received more assignments.

At the same time that Maud began to flex her knowledge and skills writing in French and English about the plight of the Irish under British rule, she was attracting attention as an effective spokesperson for the Irish. Again, she made use of Lucien's connections to give interviews. For instance, she is pictured wearing pearls with an elegant coiffure on the cover of the February 11, 1892 issue of *Le Voleur illustré* ("The Illustrated Thief"), a weekly Parisian literary magazine. Balzac had once been among its luminous stable of writers. The interviewer wrote that Miss Gonne had been born and raised in Kerry, from one of the most "noble" families in Ireland. No mention was made of her father being a British army officer. Instead she was described "as the queen of parties in Dublin who yet showed great compassion for her oppressed compatriots." Turning her back on the giddy life of a debutante, the French writer reported, this beauty chose to throw in her lot with the poor of her native land. In awe of her looks and her passion, he wrote, "At a protest, she refused to be silenced by the police and narrowly escaped six months in jail. Her sentence was not executed because there are no women's prisons in England." While this is incorrect—the English *did* have women's prisons in 1892—the admiring French journalist was closer to the mark when he concluded: "The

English, always mindful of hierarchy, couldn't resolve to put this great noble woman in an ordinary prison." On many fronts, Maud was becoming a celebrated figure in Belle Époque Paris.

So was Millevoye, but for less flattering reasons. During the summer of 1893, in front of a packed crowd of fellow politicians in the National Assembly, Millevoye accused Georges Clemenceau of being a British spy. The evidence to back up Millevoye's claim proved patently false, as the frazzled man pulled one piece of paper after another from his pocket as if he would finally find the proof. "Liar," shouted Clemenceau, and the assembled Chamber of Deputies began to laugh at Millevoye, who had been taken in by a hoax.

Millevoye had actually raised 30,000 francs to get his hands on the fake documents, which in the tense moment of crisis at the assembly he couldn't even find on his person. The cries of anger and outrage soon turned to guffaws and Millevoye left the assembly. Maurice Barrès, a contemporary French politician and writer, noted in amazement that Clemenceau laughed and slapped himself on his thighs in delight at the ridiculous spectacle Millevoye had made of himself in the assembly.

Millevoye's political reputation was in tatters. He had attacked the most prominent political leader in France without first checking whether the forged documents he had bought were real. The seller had lied to Millevoye about his employment at the British Embassy and had used stolen British Embassy notepaper to write his list of French politicians in the pay of the British.

When, a few years later, the prestigious executive editor post at the right-wing newspaper *La Patrie* opened up, Maud urged Millevoye to apply. She thought it would take his mind off the scandal and help rebuild his reputation. She was right because she had good instincts for public relations. He got the job, and then Maud began to write for him. Gradually, Maud increased her published work to include newspapers and magazines in Belfast, Dublin, London, and New York. Her audience, both in person and on the page, was growing.

Lucien like Maud was a nationalist, but for France. If Ireland became a strong independent power and could ally herself with France against Germany, that would have been of interest to him. Otherwise Ireland itself was not. In France, Lucien supported the Army and the Church at the expense of the French Republic. In little more than a decade, he supported not one but three failed right-wing coups against the elected government of the Third Republic. Like many of his compatriots, he was also virulently anti-Semitic, which tied in with his view of England as France's historical enemy. He believed England was run by Anglicans, bankers, Jews, and Freemasons, an international society with elaborate, secretive ceremonies. Lucien held the hated English responsible for ending France's days of glory under Napoleon. Lucien's anti-English and anti-Semitic views were promulgated in *La Patrie* and Maud shared them. For him, regaining France's lost provinces from Germany was a priority. Eventually, for tactical reasons, his views about England changed. Maud's did not.

Chapter 5
Advocating for Amnesty

> I never willingly discouraged either a Dynamiter or a constitutionalist, a realist or a lyrical writer. My chief preoccupation was how their work could help forward the Irish separatist movement.
>
> —*The Autobiography of Maude Gonne*

While Millevoye kept his hand in French politics as a newspaper editor and voluble critic of the Third Republic, Maud's Irish focus never wavered. She discovered a new theme: aged twenty-seven, she raised Her distinctive speaking voice on behalf of imprisoned Irish nationalists whom she called "political prisoners" because, to her, committing violent acts for Ireland was noble. In London on one of her whirlwind visits, my dear Mr. Yeats, as Maud then addressed him, brought her along to a meeting of the Amnesty Association of Great Britain. It had formed in 1892 under the leadership of Dr. Mark Ryan, its chair, and from Ryan she learned about the plight of Irish political prisoners—then only men—in English jails.

With her usual passionate enthusiasm, Maud became active in fundraising and speaking about the imprisoned Irishmen, called "Dynamitards" in the press. Dynamite, invented in 1867, had been their weapon of choice. The once young men were growing old in jail under the Treason Felony Act of 1848, especially designed by the British to deal with "The Irish dynamiters," many of whom trained and radicalized in the United States. The law made seditious acts

high treason, rather than misdemeanors, and the men were imprisoned for "levying war upon the Queen."

As punishment for their 1880s bombing campaign in Britain
targeting important historic buildings, such as the Tower of London
and the Houses of Parliament, the imprisoned Irishmen had to do
hard labor in Portland, an island prison. Irish nationalists believed
the dynamiters were treated especially harshly because they were
Irish. For instance, Tom Clarke, one of the jailed men and an important figure in the Irish nationalist movement, thought the system-
atic abuse of Irish prisoners was designed to destroy them or to
drive them mad, whichever came first: " 'Who next?' was the terrible question that haunted us day and night." The British argued that
innocent civilians had been hurt in the bombings of state buildings
and national treasures, so the Irishmen deserved their cruel punishment. The British considered the men to be terrorists.

To Maud, these "terrorists" were heroes. She thought force a
necessary tool to sever the ties between Great Britain and Ireland.
Looking back as a lifelong activist, Maud wrote: "More and more
I realised that Ireland could rely only on force . . . and that it was
absurd to say that any Irishman, whatever he did, had committed
a crime against England or against civilisation." She thought it her
duty to raise money for appeals, to publicize Irish imprisonment in
English jails, and to help support their families.

Dr. Ryan suggested Maud visit the jailed men to see their condition firsthand, and she immediately acted on his suggestion.
Knowing she wouldn't be allowed to visit under her own name, Maud
used the stationery of London-based Uncle William and asked for
permission to visit Portland prisoners using her formal given name,
Edith Gonne. Describing herself as an emissary from the men's families, she asked that she be allowed to bring them personal messages.
Her subterfuge worked. In her memoir, she never mentions if she had
actual messages for the men; my assumption is that she did not. Her

goal was to see the conditions of the men's imprisonment for herself and be their voice to the outside world. In that, she succeeded.

In 1892 she traveled to Portland Prison, the grim prison on an island off the coast of Dorset, England. The prisoners quarried stones to build the Portland breakwater. The stone wall had been built to protect the massive buildings against the implacable forces of wind and tide. In this bleak outpost, the Irishmen were allowed one twenty-minute visit every four months. Since the prisoners' families lived far away and had little or no income without their men, there were no visits. Many had seen no one from outside the Portland Prison since their incarceration a decade earlier.

"It was exactly like the cage of wild animals at the zoo," she wrote in her memoir. Like the evicted families in Donegal, these men admired their beautiful, empathetic visitor. She gave them hope, predicting when each would be released and in what order. For some, like Dr. Thomas Gallagher, arrested in 1883, it was too late. He had gone insane and, once released, spent the remainder of his life in an asylum. Maud settled another prisoner, James Cunningham, arrested in 1885, into the care of Bowie, her old nurse. According to a story in *United Ireland*, Maud was hugely responsible for shaping public opinion about these "forgotten" men, and helped secure their release: "The movement of sympathy with Irish wrongs which Miss Gonne has created in France is still a growing and gathering power. A few months ago the number of articles in the French papers upon Miss Gonne and her work had reached 2,000." The inventive Yeats, her suitor, was the source for that number, sending it in a letter to a writer and editor friend who included it in the *United Ireland* article. It is impossible to verify that claim.

Regardless of the actual number of articles about her and her work, with Millevoye's help Maud generated fantastic publicity for the Irish political prisoners she visited. For instance, *Le Gaulois* gave her a front-page story where she was quoted as saying, "While thieves and assassins are liberally given [permission] on determined days, for their parents and friends to visit, our poor Irish who have committed no other crime than to demand with a loud voice, the emancipation of their country are sequestered, isolated and stopped from all commerce with their fellow human beings." The obviously smitten reporter described Maud's expressive eyes as being "changeable like the sea, at times turquoise blue, at others grey like steel," and described how when telling the story of the men in Portland prison, "her voice trembled and her eyes filled with tears."

She excelled at publicizing these men's imprisonment. *Le Figaro* noted in June 1893: "Following revelations by Miss Maud Gonne on the atrocities in Portland prison, the English government decided to release [James] Gilbert who is '*a toute extrémité* ,'"—at the point of death.

The released men showed their gratitude to Maud in a variety of ways. For instance, after John Daly left Portland Prison, he became a local hero in his hometown of Limerick where he was elected mayor. At his swearing in ceremony, he gave Maud Gonne and his fellow prisoner Tom Clarke an honorary "freedom of the city" award. Lore has it that Daly gave Maud an old French coin and a bullet to remember the failed 1798 Irish Rebellion, in which the French joined the Irish fighting the loyalists and the British. Although Maud, the former debutante, had no use for her diamonds as an adult other than to sell them for cash to feed Irish children, she had these mementos made into a brooch that she wore with pride.

The French press seemingly couldn't get enough of the tall, strikingly attractive woman in her late twenties who spoke their language like a native. *Le Revue Mondaine Illustré*, in an 1892 piece, described how "Miss Gonne is a woman of heart in the biggest sense of the word: good and generous to a fault. She is filled with courage and a will that men might envy." Breathlessly, the French papers reported when she had pneumonia or when she went to meet with important Irish nationalists such as Timothy Harrington and Michael Davitt in Luxembourg. "Miss Maud Gonne is thin," one journalist noted, but "though frail in appearance, she contains a virile energy like one of Michelangelo's angels." Throughout her long life, not just while she lived in Paris, Maud lobbied and spoke for the rights of political prisoners in an increasingly fractured Ireland. Although she began such work as a young woman extolling arguably terrorist acts for Mother Ireland, she progressed to working for prison reform for all prisoners, arguing that "few people would be criminals if they were happy . . . That the actual prison system does not cure them or act as a deterrent is proved from the way the prison population is returned again and again to jail. Once a criminal, always a criminal is the result of the English system."

Following the establishment of the Irish Republic in 1922, she pointed out the irony of the new Irish Republican government using the same tools of detainment to control their newly minted, recalcitrant citizens that the hated English government had. She predicted the new republic would not prosper until it stopped mimicking the policies of its former oppressor. Maud believed in an Ireland that treated all prisoners decently and afforded all citizens due process. She decried the Coercion Act in a 1938 article called "Prison Bars," arguing that it "empowers any policeman to arrest any citizen on suspicion without formulating what he suspects of him." She worked ceaselessly to improve the conditions of political prisoners in Irish jails in the Republic. Her ideas for prison reform were radical and remain so today. In 1919, she wrote:

> Prisons should be sanitary, prisoners should be well fed, work there should be; gardens and farms should be attached so as to make them as far as possible self-supporting . . . the work should not be punitive, it should never be useless; recreation should be provided and intercourse allowed, though I think probably the presence of some safe person who would turn the conversation into harmless channels would be necessary.

It seemed her heart was big enough to include common criminals as well as prisoners of conscience. She believed all prisoners should be treated humanely. Posing an existential question, she wrote: "It is hard to understand the mentality of gaolers. If a political party decides to use its power to jail opponents, surely there is no reason for ill-treating them."

Her criticism remains as potent today as it was ninety years ago. What do we expect the terrorists we jail to do after they serve their sentence? To become civil law-abiding citizens? Our approach to criminals in the United States is equally problematic. We, too, have a very high rate of recidivism. Once again, Maud Gonne was ahead of her time in speaking out about human rights issues that remain important.

Chapter 6
Two Lovers Against Dreyfus

In 1894, a dark French undercurrent bubbled to the surface during the arrest and trials of Captain Alfred Dreyfus. It affected everyone in Paris, including the two lovers Maud and Lucien. To each the personal was political, and vice versa. During the Dreyfus Affair this played out in different ways for the politically driven lovers.

Captain Dreyfus was Jewish and he was framed for treason, specifically for selling War Ministry secrets to the Germans. With his arrest, anti-Semitism, dormant for a time, reared its ugly head. The whole of France polarized around those who were for and against Dreyfus. Dreyfus was tried and convicted to life in prison. The French newspaper *La Libre Parole*, edited by Édouard Drumont, founder of the anti-Semitic League of France, showcased Dreyfus the Jew's arrest as a way to prove that, by definition, all French Jews were disloyal. Drumont was a newspaperman and a political colleague of Lucien Millevoye. Both men were virulently anti-Semitic. Lucien used his position as editor of *La Patrie* to help damn Dreyfus. To him, there was no question of Drefyus's guilt. The only question was his sentence.

Maud Gonne, too, was stained by anti-Semitism. During the Dreyfus Affair, it may have been as fashionable to speak out about the captain's guilt as it was to wear Maud's distinctive Parisian hats. However, since Maud was so vocal in defending the underdog in Ireland, it shocked me that she too condemned Dreyfus simply because he was a Jew. Throughout her long life, in letters and in print, she railed against Jews and the Jewish conspiracy with banks to keep the Irish in thrall to the British Empire. She wrote an article, "Foreign Correspondent," published in the *United Irishman* in which she said:

> The liberation of the traitor Dreyfus immediately after his re-condemnation has been the last stroke . . . no French institution is now safe from the domination of the agents of the synagogue.

Anti-Semites thought that Jews controlled both public policy and banks. She was against his release. By 1899, Dreyfus had spent five years in prison on Devil's Island in French Guiana, South America. Then an investigation opened by the new chief of counterespionage, Georges Picquart, identified the real traitor: a French Army major, Ferdinand Esterhazy. He had given War Ministry documents to the Germans. High-ranking military men suppressed the new evidence. After a two-day trial, a military court unanimously acquitted Esterhazy, who fled to England. The Army then arrested Picquart, based on more forged documents.

After this judicial farce, Émile Zola, the famous French novelist, playwright, and journalist decided to use his talents to try and influence public opinion. With the encouragement of Clemenceau, the increasingly well-known politician and publisher, Zola wrote a front-page letter in Clemenceau's paper *L'Aurore*, printed on January 13, 1898. The letter was addressed to Félix Faure, president of France. "J'accuse," I accuse, he wrote, and it was Clemenceau's brilliant eye-catching ploy to make that the title of Zola's manifesto. Zola accused the generals in the War Office of concealing the truth and of acquitting Esterhazy. He accused the French press of being the creatures of the War Office and misleading the public. *L'Aurore* sold some 300,000 copies on the first day, ten times normal circulation. It was a huge success, but Zola was prosecuted for libel.

During Zola's trial in Paris, Lucien's tall figure could be seen in the audience accompanied by Jules Guérin, another journalist and notorious political and public anti-Semite. They were followed around by half a dozen thugs with "clenched fists and eyes full of menace," according to an eyewitness account by Raphaël Viau. The trial was ugly. Men "who in their ordinary lives, had no spot on their reputations, prepared to spit on Zola, if they could get close enough ... 'Down with Zola, down with the Jews,' they howled like dogs."

Zola, pronounced guilty, and sentenced to a year in prison, fled to England, but he had turned public opinion in favor of the Dreyfusards, as Dreyfus supporters were known. Meanwhile, also swinging public opinion in the captain's favor, Major Hubert-Joseph Henry, an intelligence officer, confessed to forging the documents that implicated Picquart. Major Henry was jailed. Disgraced, his reputation in ruins, he committed suicide in military prison.

The rising tide of public opinion questioning his guilt led to Dreyfus's second trial. In the summer of 1899, Dreyfus was brought back to Paris from Devil's Island. Maud objected. She thought him a traitor. Others who agreed with her took violent action. A lawyer who was a member of Dreyfus's defense team was shot in the back. He almost died during the second trial. While the lawyer was recuperating, a delay was asked for by the defendant's counsel. It was refused. The trial proceeded as planned, and for a second time Dreyfus was court-martialed and convicted, but with a reduced ten-year sentence. Days after the trial ended, on September 20, 1899, Dreyfus received an official pardon from the new French president, Émile Loubet. Sickened almost to the point of death by the conditions of his solitary imprisonment, Dreyfus was persuaded to accept the pardon by his brother. Even in his weakened state, Dreyfus insisted on continuing to fight for exoneration, and the return of his military rank. In 1906, a civilian court reversed his previous convictions. After twelve tumultuous years, Captain Dreyfus was reinstated in the army and awarded the Legion of Honor.

The Dreyfus Affair split families, and the country, into bitterly warring factions. Marcel Proust and his brother Robert, then in their twenties, both living in Paris, were Dreyfusards. Their French Catholic father was firmly in the anti-Dreyfus camp, though his wife, the mother of his two boys, was Jewish.

Maud's opinion didn't budge even after Dreyfus was exonerated in 1906. More than twenty years later, in 1927, she wrote Yeats:

My dear Willie:

In the old days when you were a Dreyfusard you used to think it fine the thesis 'Better France perish, than one man suffer injustice'!

I held that Dreyfus was an uninteresting jew & too much money was spent on his cause for it to be an honest cause ...

Being a nationalist, I sympathized with French nationalists who objected to the Jews & international finance interfering in their country & upsetting their institutions.

Maud and Lucien remained strongly set against Dreyfus. The Affair was a significant milestone in their "alliance" because it showed what kind of French nationalists they were: for the French military and the clergy, against French Jews, English bankers, and even Freemasonry, which they also believed had been infiltrated by Jews.

Why or how Maud developed her anti-Semitism remains a puzzle. While of course there was a centuries-old tradition of anti-Semitism in both Catholicism and Protestantism, there were few Jews in Ireland when Maud was a child, and in Europe her encounters would have been limited to families of the same background as she, in other words, Protestant English or Protestant Anglo-Irish families. The Anglo-Irish, as they were called, were Ireland's ruling class. There's no evidence in any of the family letters written during Maud's childhood, that she, her father Tommy or her sister Kathleen met, remarked on, or knew any Jews.

But anti-Semitism certainly pervaded Maud's adult life. By her thirties, Maud left a written record of how she felt about Jews; by then, she had met some. In 1898 her anti-Semitism was a reason she gave Yeats for leaving the Order of the Golden Dawn, the secretive London order devoted to magic, ritual, and the occult. She wrote that her cousin May, "like myself, was rather repelled by the Semitic aspect of the teaching."

Among the religious lore delved into by the Order of the Golden Dawn was the Kabbalah, the Jewish mystical tradition. Members of the order were required to take on new names in Hebrew, and Maud clearly didn't like the use of those names. In another letter to Yeats, she complained about "the proximity of Jew bankers" in the gaming rooms of the Aix-les-Bains spa; she then avoided them even though she liked "gaming." Perhaps Maud's views on Jews were absorbed as a young woman, when she first met Lucien in Royat and formed "the alliance."

During the years the Dreyfus Affair dragged on through the courts and the French press, Lucien was a regular at the trials. He watched the proceedings every day, heckled the Dreyfusards and reported on the trial for *La Patrie*. Maud's energy, in contrast, remained focused on the cause of Irish independence. Although she called herself a Republican in France and in Ireland, she meant something different by that term in each country. To her, being an Irish Republican meant she worked steadfastly, throughout her long life, to publicize and help sever Ireland's political ties with England. In France saying she was a Republican meant in reality that she, like Lucien, was a French nationalist who supported leaders whose power came from the backing of the army and the church, rather than the elected representatives of the Republic.

Her position on the Dreyfus Affair was consistent with her particular brand of French nationalism. In Paris, where most French

Jews were and remain concentrated today, Maud was not unusual in her anti-Semitism. However, anti-Semitism had taken an insidious turn with the emancipation of French Jews beginning with the 1789 Revolution and continuing on into the mid-nineteenth century. That's when the last remnants of medieval legislation denying Jews full French citizenship and access to the professions were lifted. Jews were then recognized as French citizens, just like Christians or Muslims.

Christian dogma frowned on moneylending, or "usury," and charging high interest rates on loans. That meant believing Christians did not engage in money lending for profit. So did Jewish theology prohibit it, but rabbis allowed the practice outside the community. Only after the Protestant Reformation did Jean Calvin develop his dogma permitting Protestants to charge interest for lending money. This radical new Protestant belief drove the development of the Swiss banking industry. But Catholic Church dogma continued to preach against usury as a mortal sin, and stated that those practicing it would burn in hell. (Neither did Islam allow Muslims to lend money with interest, though Islam permits loans financed based on real assets, just not on borrowed cash.)

So, for centuries, since it was condemned by other major religions, European Jews amassed considerable experience and profit lending money and financing new businesses. With the inventions of the nineteenth century, among them steam and locomotion, Jews financed increasingly grand industrial projects. Modern anti-Semites, among them Maud, blamed "Jew bankers" for the rise of the materialist capitalist world. This too unfortunately made Maud modern; for her, as for many Parisians of the Belle Époque, anti-Semitism was the default mindset.

When I discovered that Maud Gonne not only was a lifelong anti-Semite, but her daughter was one too, I was horrified. Maud's daughter Iseult's anti-Semitism went further. She married a young novelist, Francis Stuart, who shared her anti-Semitic views and felt so strongly about them that he later abandoned her and their children for a woman in Berlin where he worked as a radio host for the Nazi radio station Irland-Redaktion in Berlin from 1942 to 1944.

Both my parents were Jewish, but they celebrated Christian holidays, not Jewish ones. We never went to temple. My father, after my mother left him for another man, married a succession of WASPs. His third wife, a Mayflower WASP, thought a big reason he married her was because of her WASP background. That's what she told me. Then, with her as his wife, he could get into the Connecticut social clubs that had ostracized him and my mother as a couple of Jews. A new WASP spouse of old New England stock turned the social tide for both of them.

When my sister had four healthy children, my father examined them to see if they had "Jewish" noses, like his. To his relief, none of them did. When I told him about a friend's work as a documentary filmmaker, interviewing four women friends who had survived the Bergen-Belsen concentration camp by saving each other's lives, my father said she had chosen a bad subject because "we shouldn't dwell on the Holocaust." To do so would bring more attention to Jews. Presumably, he believed such attention on Jews would inevitably give rise to persecution. My father confessed that when he was growing up, "it wasn't a good thing to be identified as a Jew." I can only speculate that he meant being openly identified as Jewish limited his opportunities and subjected him to the kind of harassment he experienced in college. After I read in his yearbook that he had transferred from one college to another, he reluctantly revealed he had done so because of anti-Semitism. He wouldn't elaborate.

My mother's anti-Semitism was subtle. She made herself into a historian after the last of her three children graduated from college. In the process of writing three books, she became an apologist for Stalin. She further insisted that Hitler didn't treat the Jews any differently than he did the Slavs.

Cut to decades ago, when as a self-conscious teen I wondered if I was pretty or if my nose was too big for my face. My mother told me I could get it fixed if I wanted. I didn't. What I wanted was her reassurance that my nose was fine for my small oval face. I neither understood my mother's Jewish self-loathing nor her desire to assimilate. When I asked if there was anything positive that could be attributed to what was to me the mystery of being a Jew, she paused for a long time. Finally, she said, "Well, Jews are supposed to be smart." The man she left my father for was an uber-WASP from Boston. "Why," he would ask me when he'd drunk his evening cocktail, "do you think Jews are so hated? What is the reason?"

As an adult I had the satisfaction of having an adult bat-mitzvah. In a big room at my local Jewish community center, surrounded by friends and family, my rabbi welcomed me into the world as a responsible Jewish adult.

I was shocked and dismayed to discover that my heroine, the tender-hearted Maud Gonne—so sensitive that after she once shot and killed a lark, from then on only "aimed at fir cones"—was a lifelong anti-Semite.

Chapter 7
Star-Crossed Lovers or Just Good Friends?

During the same period that Maud became an activist for Irish prisoners in British jails lecturing throughout France, England, and the United States, she engaged in an elaborate dance of engagement and retreat with Yeats. Her ardent admirer called his a "perplexed wooing," perhaps the understatement of the century. After his first proposal, in 1891, when he was twenty-five and she was twenty-four, he waited seven years before proposing again. He was to propose twice more before he finally gave up.

At the age of thirty-one, he at last lost his virginity to an attractive married woman named Olivia Shakespear, no relation to the famous bard. Olivia was unhappy with her husband, a man fourteen years older. She met Yeats at a London dinner party where she was brought along as a guest of her cousin Lionel Johnson, a poet and friend of Yeats. Olivia and Yeats were acquainted for two years before their relationship developed into an amorous one. She, the more experienced of the two awkward lovers, kissed him first on a train.

With Olivia in mind, Yeats moved out of his family's home in Bedford Park. Given the beatification of family in Victorian society, it would have been impossible for Yeats to arrange to meet a woman, let alone a married woman, in his family's home for a romantic encounter. Instead, in February 1896, he moved into two rented rooms of his own in Woburn Buildings, in the Bloomsbury district of London. His small bedroom and large sitting room were above a cobbler's shop. In London, storefronts like the cobbler's had become increasingly popular, making it pleasant for visitors and residents to stroll through

London's sprawling, ever expanding network of streets. Yeats finally had a decent place of his own to live.

Together Yeats and Shakespear purchased a bed: "I remember an embarrassed conversation in the presence of some Tottenham Court shop man upon the width of the bed—every inch increased the expense." However uncomfortable he was, Yeats went ahead and made the purchase. For a brief interlude he experienced the giddiness of a frisky, satisfied lover. He expressed it poetically, writing the poem "He Gives His Beloved Certain Rhymes," for the dark-haired Olivia.

However, Maud after months of silence reappeared in Yeats's life that autumn, perhaps because even after the birth of their second child, her relationship with Lucien continued to flounder. Lucien had asked her to have an affair with another man to further his political goals. She refused. The source for this tidbit of information was Yeats and Anna MacBride White, Maud's granddaughter. Anna White grew up with her grandmother, living in the same home. Both Yeats and White attributed this anecdote to Maud but gave no further details so it is difficult to know if this behavior was out of the ordinary for a French politician of the Belle Époque. Maud and Lucien clearly viewed their relationship differently. To her it was a partnership "to the death," as she melodramatically promised, with her hand in his, as a young woman. She selected him as the father of two of her children. She boldly made the first move. It was she who talked to him first at the spa at Royat when they met, and she who brought about their reconciliation when she wanted to have another child in Paris after their baby died of meningitis. Being an upper-class, financially independent woman made her bold.

In November 1895 Maud wrote the ever-enamored Yeats that, while entertaining guests in her hotel room, he had come to her in an occult vision. No one else could see him, and she realized it was an apparition. Was everything all right? Had he had a similar occult vision that they were together? She believed she was intuitive and had second sight. On this occasion, I agree.

Yeats had invited Olivia Shakespear and a friend of hers to tea, but he'd been thinking hard of Maud Gonne and became distracted. He walked out to buy a cake and came back with the cake but no door key. He had to find a man to climb in through a window to let him and his guests in. When Maud sensed his presence, he'd been locked out. Later that same evening he spoke for hours about his overpowering feelings for Maud to his friend Arthur Symons, a poet and the editor of Yeats's work in the London literary magazine *Savoy*.

Despite his excitement about his soon-to-be consummated affair with Olivia, Yeats couldn't give up his obsession with Maud. Together he envisioned their delving ever deeper into Irish lore and perhaps twining their bodies together as well as their minds. He'd been collecting Irish folktales, turning them into literature, as Maud encouraged him to do. In the august halls of the British Library in London he found the names of Celtic gods, and then with Maud and other members of the Golden Dawn tried to summon them up by using mescaline or hashish. They did it so often that Maud nicknamed hash, which they had first taken together in Paris in 1894, "the dream drug."

Opium and cocaine were legal in Britain, not regulated until 1920, and France had no laws on the books to control recreational drug use until 1908. Paris had a famous hashish club that included the literary luminaries of mid-nineteenth-century Paris: Charles Baudelaire, Alexandre Dumas, and Honoré de Balzac. In Paris, Yeats was continuing the literary tradition of experimenting with drugs allegedly for the sake of poetry.

Understandably, given his entanglement with Maud, Yeats's affair with Olivia flickered. It didn't last a year. By 1897 it was over. Per usual, he turned his grief about the end of his first carnal romance into a poem, "The Lover Mourns for the Loss of Love." Olivia had come to his apartment, but instead of reading her love poetry as he usually did to get in the mood for their amorous activities, he stayed at his desk writing letters. "She burst into tears. 'There is someone else in your heart,' she said. It was the breaking between us for many years."

In his autobiography, after describing the break with Olivia, Yeats records how his strong feelings for Gonne came to the fore.

> I saw much of Maud Gonne and my hope revived again. If I could go to her and prove by putting my hand into the fire til I had burned it badly, would not that make her understand that devotion like mine should (not) be lightly thrown away.... These events have no very precise date to me.

Yeats plunged into nationalist and occult activities with Maud, journeying back and forth between London, Dublin, and Paris to be with her as well as to pursue his widening circle of literary and theatrical connections. Yeats, like his perpetually broke father, borrowed money from friends and kept himself on a strict budget. But by the close of the 1890s, he was making a small amount of money as a journalist, poet, and editor.

After his and Maud's trip to Howth five summers earlier, he knew they shared a visceral connection with the Irish landscape. During different stages of their childhood they had both spent years in the very same picturesque village.

The rocky, green Irish seascape of Howth may have been embedded in the two young friends' psyches, fueled by the formative years they spent there. For both, their yearning for a deeper meaning in their lives was connected to their affection for the Irish countryside. They both wanted to accustom a wide audience to local folklore and to the belief that ancient Irish spirits inhabited the land. That was one way to set Ireland's culture apart from England's. As the president of the National Literary Society, their friend and contemporary Douglas Hyde expressed these same views in a speech given in Dublin in 1892, "On the Necessity for De-Anglicizing the Irish People."

All across Ireland, committed Irish nationalist intellectuals, including Maud and Yeats, embarked on a tumultuous voyage where they collaborated and helped imagine a new Irish Republic, one that hadn't existed for five hundred years. Before this new republic could become a reality, they had to dream it up. It became their collective fantasy. As Yeats brilliantly wrote of himself and his fellow nationalists in "The Stare's Nest By My Window":

We had fed the heart on fantasies,
The heart's grown brutal on the fare,
More substance in our enmities
Than in our love;

While others were working on a proposal to give Ireland its own parliament, they were creating the romantic tale of an ancient subjugated country worth fighting for. Maud realized the unique contribution Yeats could make to Ireland through his poetic genius. In November 1895 she wrote to him:

My dear Mr. Yeats,
For the honor of our country, the world must recognize you one of the Great Poets of the century. Be true to yourself & let nothing interfere with your literary work. That is surely your first duty.

Her formality in addressing him as "My dear Mr. Yeats," can be interpreted as playfully Victorian. In the spring of 1897, she wrote about his new book, *The Secret Rose*. "The language is so lovely, it is like some wonderful eastern jewel. One never tires of it—it must be heavenly to be able to express one's thoughts like that."

The two friends hatched a scheme to turn an uninhabited island named Castle Rock into a place where, in Yeats's words, they could unite "the perception of the spirit of the divine with natural beauty," and use Celtic symbols "to bring into imaginative life the old sacred spaces." Maud thought if they could "make contact with the hidden forces of the land it would give [them] strength for the freeing of Ireland."

In the summer of 1897, when not dreaming of new ways to bring Maud close, Yeats was miserable. He wrote in his autobiography, from the vantage point of fifty:

> It was a time of great personal strain and sorrow. Since my mistress had left me, no other woman had come into my life, and for nearly seven years none did. I was tortured by sexual desire and disappointed love. Often as I walked in the woods at Colle it would have been a relief to have screamed aloud. When desire became an unendurable torture, I would masturbate, and that, no matter how moderate I was, would make me ill. It never occurred to me to seek another love. I would repeat to myself again and again the last confession of Lancelot, and indeed it was my greatest pride, 'I have loved a queen beyond measure and exceeding long.'

The incident kicking off Yeats's summer of anguish occurred June 1897. What tripped up their apparent intimacy was Maud's affection for crowds, even when they were riled up and dangerous. She seemed to have a soldier's heart. She must have enjoyed the adrenaline rush of being in a crowd because throughout her long life she sought out protests, as she had done as a young woman in the memorable protests of Trafalgar Square.

That summer, Maud persuaded Yeats to leave his uncle's home in Sligo to come east to Dublin for the protests against Queen Victoria's planned Jubilee celebrations. The Jubilee was a series of events to honor the Queen's sixtieth year as reigning monarch of Britain, the longest monarch ever to rule the Empire. The British

Empire stretched east from Hong Kong, south to India, and then across the seas to Canada's westernmost provinces, giving rise to the truism that "The sun never sets on the British Empire."

As a woman opposed to British colonialism, at the height of Empire, Maud was consciously active in organizing protests against the Jubilee. When she arrived in Dublin from France, she went to lay a wreath on the grave of the Irish rebel Robert Emmet. Due to security for the upcoming Jubilee, the cemetery gate was locked. In Dublin, Maud joined forces with James Connolly, the charismatic founder of the Irish Republican Socialist Party. He asked her to speak at his open-air meeting and she agreed. It was her first experience speaking at a public meeting on city streets. According to Yeats, the crowd thrilled to hear Maud asking "in a low voice that seemed to go through the whole crowd, 'Must the graves of our dead go undecorated because Victoria has her Jubilee?' and the whole crowd went wild." Then, "with a joyous face," Maud followed Connolly in a mock funeral procession down Dame Street behind a coffin draped in black labeled "The British Empire."

Then she and Yeats went for tea in the National Club. Suddenly, they could hear the loud noise of fights breaking out between demonstrators and the police. Yeats asked a man to lock the door so Maud could not rush out to see what was happening. He didn't want her to get hurt. The crowd was dangerous. An old woman was crushed in the melee and some two hundred people were injured and taken to the hospital.

James Connolly was arrested. The next morning Maud, who could be quite practical when it came to seeing to other people's needs rather than her own, arranged to send him breakfast in Bridewell Prison. She visited him that same day to pay his fine. Then she went to the tenement flat where his family of five was squashed together in one room and gave an update to his wife. As if she hadn't done enough to help Connolly, she persuaded her friend Tim Harrington, a lawyer as well as a politician, to defend him in court.

Once she was back in London on January 1897, Maud let her "dear Mr. Yeats" know she was furious. She wrote:

> Our friendship must indeed be strong for me not to hate you, for you made me do the most cowardly thing I have ever done in my life. It is quite absurd to say I should have reasoned and given explanations.
>
> Do you ask a soldier for explanations on the battlefield of course it is only a very small thing a riot & a police charge but the same need for *immediate action* is there—there is no time to give explanations....
>
> You have a higher work to do—With me it is different I was born to be in the midst of a crowd.

Had she been part of the crowd, Maud claimed, she could have saved the woman's life. That's impossible to know, but as Maud repeatedly demonstrated, she disliked her actions being controlled by a man. She hadn't liked it when Millevoye followed her to Ireland and demanded she return home. She refused. Nor did she like Yeats limiting her freedom. However, by the next fall, the breach between the two old friends healed.

Yeats must have complained about the formality of her letters because she wrote on September 6, 1897: "My letters are formal perhaps—as my manner is generally, but they are not unkind." One month later, she addressed him more warmly as: "My dear Friend." So, they continued their baroque dance of engagement and retreat, twirling forward and back across the vast dance floor of their lives. In 1896–1897 the two were in constant motion, separately and together, physically covering a lot of territory.

Together Maud and Yeats went to Manchester, England for a commemoration of Wolfe Tone's uprising of 1798. Then Maud went west to Ballina, Ireland, the site of his 1798 Irish–French battle against the British. In October 1897 through the beginning of 1898, she toured the United States and spoke all over the country to raise money for Wolfe Tone's memorial. Many in her audience were Irish immigrants, newly minted American citizens. They had living memories of the Great Hunger, which had funneled a million men and women across the Atlantic, and they were nostalgic for their Irish homeland. The American press loved Maud. In print, the *New York Herald* called her "the Irish Joan of Arc," and trumpeted, "Miss Maud Gonne comes to this country in the cause of the Emerald Isle."

In 1897 the irony of Maud's embracing the moniker suggested by her lover Lucien was profound. She was neither saint, nor warrior, nor teenager. By then a mother in her early thirties, she had buried one child out of wedlock (listed as "parents unknown" on his death certificate) and given birth to another. None of this fit in with the mores of Victorian society in London, the puritanical United States, or the rising tide of Irish Catholic nationalism in Ireland. The same "Irish patriots" who abandoned Parnell would surely have skewered Maud too, if the truth about her domestic arrangements in Paris were known.

For years, rumors swirled about Maud Gonne to the lovesick, yearning poet. She heard some about him too. In May 1896, she wrote him that she heard that he had married a widow, but discounted it. "I thought we were sufficiently friends for you to have told me." He in turn, heard "stories" about her being a wicked, dissolute woman for years and batted away the rumors. One story Yeats heard identified him as her secret lover and claimed they had aborted an illegitimate child. Even though he knew nothing explicitly, Yeats had an intuitive jealous hunch about the French Boulangist "friend" who had arranged Maud's first speaking engagements in France.

Yeats explained: "I heard much scandal about her but dismissed . . . one persistent story I put away with the thought, 'She would have told me if it were true.'" Of course, she didn't. Nor did he tell her about his first love affair with the married Olivia Shakespear. While both Yeats and Gonne were remarkable standouts in their time for different reasons, they were human beings of the Victorian era. Both were discreet about their relationships outside the sanctity of marriage. Each of them was involved in an adulterous relationship with a married person. Neither knew about the other's.

In 1897, after the debacle in the Dublin tearoom, Yeats spent what was to be the first of many productive summers recovering physically and emotionally while visiting Lady Gregory at her estate at Coole Park in County Galway. Her house was surrounded by a thousand acres of forest and a lake complete with swans. When Yeats was brought into the wealthy, elegant widow's orbit by their mutual friend, the writer and British Arts and Crafts Movement textile designer William Morris, it was a happy moment for both. Yeats, then thirty-one, and Lady Augusta, forty-four, formed a life-long bond, one that enriched their lives and Irish culture—which the two rooted around for in libraries in the countryside and ultimately helped create. Separately and together they collected Irish folklore, preserving folktales in literature, as opposed to relying on the spoken word and generations of oral Irish storytelling. Together they formed Ireland's first national theater, the Abbey Theatre in Dublin; they both wrote a number of plays that graced the Abbey stage.

What Lady Gregory thought of Maud when finally introduced was: "A shock to me—for instead of beauty I saw a death's head." Lady Gregory was civil and even gave valuable advice to Maud, based on what they had in common: being rich women in a time when the laws were kinder to men. Lady Gregory knew herself to be part of the ruling Protestant landlord class in Ireland and rightly realized that despite Maud's politics, she too was a member of the British upper classes and vulnerable to the misogynist laws of their era.

Meanwhile, Lady Gregory had to endure many more letters from Yeats about Maud. As she realized, like the good friend and mentor she became, Yeats was obsessed with her. The word "obsessed" comes from the Latin word for obsession, meaning "a besieging."

For example, one's heart and mind are flooded with thoughts and feelings for another person. One can't stop thinking of them. For an artist, if he, she, or they can transform their obsession into their chosen art form it can be useful. Certainly, Yeats turned his fixation on Maud into some of the most gorgeous lyric poems written in English in the twentieth century. On the other hand, an obsession can interfere with the rest of one's life and prevent one from moving on into another actual, rather than yearned for, relationship.

Yeats's obsession with Maud, and Maud's entanglement with the morally rather despicable Lucien (admittedly, the records against Millevoye are biased, as the sources are Yeats, Maud, Iseult, and contemporaries such as Clemenceau who scorned Lucien for his right-wing politics) seemed strangely familiar because of my own experience with obsession. Like Maud, when I was twenty, I had a sudden death in my family. Hers was her adored father dying at the relatively young age of fifty. Mine was my sister.

She was the middle of three sisters and I was the youngest, the baby. She was the star athlete of our family, of our school, and of our city. A gymnast, she did aerial front and back walkovers on the balance beam and she excelled academically. I was often called her name by teachers who had Gail in their class first. When she was twenty and on leave from Princeton, a New York doctor diagnosed her as schizophrenic. To capsulize, her remaining three years were dreadful: in and out of hospitals for medical and psychological treatment, and attempted suicide. I looked after her because I adored her. She was such fun and, in our family, she mothered and protected me as my own mother did not. Preoccupied with their divorce, and other lovers, my parents were clueless as to what to do about Gail. My oldest sister, then at Harvard Business School, didn't want to be involved. That left it to me to organize her care because no one else in our family took it on. I failed to help her because her illness was acute, her unraveling rapid. A series of unfortunate events battered her fragile psyche until she finally "succeeded" in killing herself.

She jumped out a window of my father's apartment on Park Avenue, ending her life at twenty-three. I was twenty.

I sympathize with Maud's choice of Lucien Millevoye and her standing by him for twelve years despite his infidelities. In hindsight, I think my choice of lover as a young woman was equally misguided, though on the surface someone could be pardoned for thinking it might work. We graduated from the same college, and he was smart and charming, but I fell in love with him because he was the first man I could talk to about my sister. He related to my loss because he had experienced one too, the searing pain of his glamorous fast-living best friend overdosing on coke after an older brother died. For over a decade, this man was my lover and my confidante. He was a terrible boyfriend, cheating on every woman he ever called his girlfriend, which for a few months included me. I hung on because I thought he understood the profundity of my loss and I could unpack it with him. He was the only one who wanted to hear the terrible story of Gail's last three years. No one else asked. He was very smart and loved theater, as I do. Being involved, even obsessed with him into my thirties is unutterably painful to recall as I turned down other attractive, smart men who wanted nothing more than to be able to love a woman and eventually support a family as writers, among other "risky" professions. Their orientation was towards a partnership. The man I latched onto was a philanderer who prided himself on his conquests. The men I spurned each succeeded in his chosen profession and found a partner with whom to have children and raise a family. It saddens me immensely to think I wasted twelve of my best fertility years on this fellow. I related to Maud's long relationship with a man who didn't value her as she deserved.

On the flipside of obsession, I myself was the subject of one so I was fascinated by Yeats's long obsession with Maud. Like her, I was the object of a lifelong obsession by another undergraduate. He fell in love with me sophomore year, when he saw me perform the lead in *The Madwoman of Chaillot*. It took forty years for him to tell me so.

In that time, I'd divorced. He'd moved on, married, and had children, but still carried a torch for me. What so intrigued me about the relationship between Maud and Yeats was the connection between love, friendship, art, and obsession. For myself, the obsession of my fellow alumnus developed in a more conventionally satisfying way. The more I get to know him, the more I realized how well suited we are, though since life is complicated, it continues to unfold.

As for Yeats and Maud, my sadness for them could be limited by my own conventional thinking. What they forged in the Victorian era was remarkable and nourished them both. Concerning Maud and Yeats's thirty-eight-year relationship, many critics and scholars have weighed in with their opinions about this strange one-hundred-year-old love story. I believe it was symbiotic and that both, for very different reasons, were unable to make a conventional, domestic partnership with someone of the opposite sex.

Yeats alchemized his current of feelings for Maud and shaped them into poetry. In "Words," he writes:

I had this thought a while ago,
'My darling cannot understand
What I have done, or what would do
in this blind bitter land.'

And I grew weary of the sun
Until my thoughts cleared up again,
Remembering that the best I have done
Was done to make it plain;

That every year I have cried, 'At length
My darling understands it all,
Because I have come into my strength
And words obey my call';

> That had she done so who can say
> What would have shaken from the sieve?
> I might have thrown poor words away
> And been content to live.

In the Victorian era, as Yeats demonstrated, a male artist could use a woman as muse. As he makes explicit in this poem, his yearned for love was an impetus to write poetry and become a master at it. If Maud had been available to be his wife:

> I might have thrown poor words away
> And been content to live.

From Maud's point of view, the relationship was reciprocal. She could count on Yeats when she was in trouble, which was often. For example, in 1902 she was maligned and accused of being a French spy by Frank Hugh O'Donnell, a nationalist who Yeats called "the Mad Rogue." Yeats took action, spoke against the man and prevented his getting a seat in the Irish Party. Another embittered nationalist, Charles MacCarthy Teeling, ousted from the Young Ireland Society of London because of his violent temper (having thrown a chair at the chairman, John O'Leary) set about slandering Maud Gonne. He told anyone who'd listen that she was a spy for the English government and "a vile abandoned woman who has had more than one illegitimate child." At Maud's request, Yeats wrote a letter attacking Teeling and explaining he'd been expelled from the Young Ireland Society of London, of which Yeats was president. Yeats's Young Ireland Society organized and coordinated commemorative celebrations for Wolfe Tone's failed uprising of 1798. Maud depended on Yeats to quell rumors and speak up for her, and in the course of their long relationship, he only turned her down once.

By 1898 the striking-looking couple—he with his mop of dark hair and glasses, in a velvet jacket or cape, and she statuesque in

Parisian couture—had known each other for almost a decade. When seen together by friends and colleagues they were much admired. Ella Young, one of their acolytes, wrote:

> I see her standing with W. B. Yeats the poet in front of Whistler's Miss Alexander in the Dublin gallery where some pictures by Whistler are astonishing a select few. These two delight the bystanders more than the pictures. Everyone stops looking at the canvas and maneuvers himself or herself into a position to watch these two. They are almost of equal height. Yeats has a dark, romantic cloak about him; Maud Gonne has a dress that changes color as she moves. They pay no attention to the stir they are creating; they stand there discussing the picture.

In December 1898, Maud took Yeats by surprise when they saw each other in Dublin. First, she told him that she had dreamed that they were married. Then she kissed him on the lips, the first time they had ever kissed with their "bodily mouths." Then, taking a big step, she revealed her secret life with Millevoye. Whatever he intuited about her relationship with Millevoye and with the baby who died, he seemed to have remained oblivious in his conscious mind. Discovering that the rumors he'd been batting away like pesky flies were true must have been traumatic. To his utter dismay, he learned that his goddess, his Helen of Troy, had been in a liaison with a married Frenchman for twelve long years while he'd been pursuing her. Far from being chaste, she'd had two children. The affair had ended, she told Yeats.

Backstory: shattered by her belief that he had broken their political "alliance," Maud broke off amorous relations with Millevoye. In her memoir, she makes the decision sound political. She explains that he permitted another, younger woman (his current mistress, though she doesn't spell that out) to publish an article in the newspaper he edited, *La Patrie*. The young chanteuse argued in the piece that Germany was the sole enemy of France. That meant Lucien was no longer Maud's partner "to the death" in the fight against England.

Maud concluded her revelation by telling Yeats that, since her break with Millevoye, she had loved no other. According to Yeats scholar Deirdre Toomey, Maud made the first move with Yeats both verbally and physically. She told him that she dreamed that they were married, then she kissed the sensitive poet full on the lips, and revealed that she loved no one else. Toomey believes that by acting and speaking in this way, Maud was proposing to Yeats without actually saying the crucial words.

What must he have thought, this still-impoverished Victorian poet, to the revelation that his adored one had an illegitimate daughter? If he married Maud, he would be that child's stepfather. How could he afford it? Could his ego handle the reality of her past, her superior fiscal power, her sexual experience, and the existence of a child?

For their entire relationship, he kept his fiscal independence and his pride intact, borrowing from other friends but never Maud. If he married her, would he have to accept an allowance, move to Paris, and take on Iseult as his own? The thoughts coursing through his brain must have been overwhelming. She, in turn, seemed to expect the chivalrous romantic poet, who for years had dogged her footsteps, to kiss her back and propose. It is my opinion that if he had done so at that delicate moment, she would have accepted.

The shocked poet didn't. For ten days, while she helped the evicted in Loughrea, west of Dublin in Galway, he wrote agonized, confused letters to his patron and friend Lady Gregory. Meanwhile, in the letters Yeats and Maud wrote each other during the week and a half that she was away, they made no mention of their feelings for one another, instead discussing their dreams. Maud dreamed of being in a white dress with Yeats (perhaps a wedding dress?), while he dreamed of her in a red dress visiting him astrally, "a somewhat threatening erotic figure, her lap full of expanding flowers." When she returned to Dublin, things between them remained confused: Yeats did finally propose to Maud but he did not reach out to her physically. Instead, he was careful to "touch her as one might a sister." No slow sensuous kisses. Poor Maud. She had made the first move and it had failed.

Lady Gregory suggested Yeats follow Maud to Paris and not leave until he had her "promise of marriage." She generously offered to fund this trip because, at last, his longed-for prize seemed within reach. Yeats refused Lady Gregory's offer with the words that he was "exhausted." The emotionally devastated poet told her "I can do no more." He retreated to the Sligo home of his favorite uncle, George Pollexfen, where he worked on more occult visions and his plans for an Irish literary theater. When he finally went to Paris in January 1899, Maud seemed to have accepted that he could be her knight in shining armor, but could not play the part of a hotblooded male.

For both Maud and Yeats, the disappointment of their first kiss on the mouth must have been devastating. It rippled outward. Maud, the captain's daughter, who deliberately taught herself to overcome childish fears, was the first to recover, moving on and entering into another romantic relationship. For Yeats, the road he traveled alone was much longer.

Chapter 8
A New Cause and a New Man: The Boer War and John MacBride

Yeats's gentle, careful behavior towards Maud, treating her as if she were a sister rather than a lover, caused her to retreat emotionally. It didn't matter that Yeats pursued Maud to Paris. At the end of January 1899 he proposed again, but Maud had moved on after her bold move in kissing him first failed to ignite an eager amorous response. Yeats reported to Lady Gregory, his keen confidante:

> I don't know whether things are well or ill with me, in some way ill, for she has been almost cold with me, though she has made it easy for me to see her. If you knew all . . . you would understand why this love has been so bitter a thing to me.

Later the same month he continued his account to the amazingly patient Lady Gregory:

> During the last months, and most of all while I have been here, she has told me the story of her life, telling gradually, in more detail, all except a few things which I can see are too painful for her to talk of and about which I do not ask her. I do not wonder that she shrinks from life.

What Yeats doesn't say is that during all the years he thought of Maud as a virginial goddess, she had a French lover. Her relationship with that man had lasted over a decade. When Yeats noted she had difficulty climbing stairs in London, it wasn't because she was ill, but because she was pregnant. Even if she told Yeats that she and Lucien no longer had sexual relations after the birth of Iseult in 1894, could he believe her? She had been lying to him for years.

Yeats and Maud traveled together from Paris to Dublin. Each then resumed the feverish pace of their activities. Both cultivated a growing coterie of followers, Yeats for his poetry and increasingly for an Irish theater that he had imagined but didn't yet exist. Maud drew crowds for her fiery speeches and her published work. It seems a miracle that neither collapsed of exhaustion before they were forty. Luckily, they both had other resources to draw on.

Maud regularly retreated to French spas for month-long rests where she walked, soaked in the hot springs, and read novels. That seemed her tonic for overwork and exhaustion. Yeats, once he discovered the magic of Lady Gregory's thousand-acre estate in Coole Park, went there to visit again and again. He wrote many poems in homage to the park and in them immortalized small beauties, such as the seven different kinds of trees in the woods. After his disappointing Paris trip in pursuit of Maud, Yeats became ill. Lady Gregory helped nurse him back to health in London by delivering homemade food and drink made by her personal chef. She did more than that: she enhanced his first independent home. When Yeats moved in, she made the flat more comfortable. She measured the windows for curtains which she presumably paid for, since she made it a habit of showering the financially-challenged poet with gifts both generous and practical. She added a leather easy chair to his study. In some ways, she was the mother the undernourished-looking thirty-five-year-old poet never had. As his many letters to Gregory attest, he treasured her.

Maud knew that Yeats's great patron was another force driving the burgeoning Irish nationalist culture movement. Over the years Maud made many close women friends, but Lady Gregory never became one. Maud was too extreme in her views for Lady Gregory, a landlord herself who defended landlord rights. For instance, she was outraged when Maud and her friend the socialist James Connolly told poor tenant farmers in Mayo that the theft of sheep and cattle during a famine was not a sin. In February 1898, the two radicals advised tenants to take what they needed from their landlords in order to survive. Yeats reported this new development to Lady Gregory. She insisted Yeats dissuade Maud from promoting such a radical view of property.

Maud didn't just promote "robbery," as Lady Gregory called it. She helped hungry families in Belderrig in County Mayo by doing a number of practical things such as setting up an organization of women to distribute oatmeal and condensed milk. To the men, she proposed the construction of a dry fish factory that would keep them working and fed in the event of another crop failure. With local officials and the parish priest, she drew up a list of demands including raising relief rates for the head of households to one shilling a day, roughly $6.48 in 2020.

Relief rates were paid to the head of households for a day's work building roads, some of which, as Maud drily noted, led nowhere. The English authorities didn't want to give away food or money for nothing. Faced with the crowds of hungry people backed by their local priests, officials (in consultation with representatives from Dublin Castle) capitulated to their modest demands for a living wage.

In January 1900, Maud geared up for her second tour of the United States. To Maud, the Irish diaspora in America was a potential source of the dollars needed to support a successful revolt in Ireland. There were some forty million Irish Americans and they had hard-earned money to give and a bitter longing for the country they had been forced to leave in order to survive. There were many more Irish in the United States than there were in Ireland, or on the continent. Cities such as Boston, Chicago, and New York had massive Irish American populations (in 1860, a quarter of New York's population) and were able to launch Irish-American political candidates. As Irish Americans thrived, they became a force in the United States and began to affect policy.

By then Maud had heard of Major John MacBride, an Irishman who went to South Africa to organize an Irish brigade to fight on behalf of the Boers. The British were determined to keep South Africa under their dominion, but the Boers (Afrikaans for "farmers") were just as determined to keep their independence. Neither party talked about the indigenous Africans presumably because they were black and considered inferior to whites. The Irish equated the Boer struggle against the British with their own. Irish members of Parliament, guided by their constituents, were unanimous in their opposition to the Boer War. The British were the most visible of all the colonial powers; they were at the height of their military power around the world, which meant they were a visible target for political criticism. As ideas of romantic nationalism spread globally, local people from Africa to India began to chafe under British rule. Romantic nationalism was the idea that geography shaped a culture, language, and people, and that those people had a right to self-determination, as opposed to the belief in the divine right of kings and the transcendence of empire.

Maud noted and applauded each and every new challenge to Britain's empire. She learned about the Indian nationalist movement as it grew and eagerly welcomed many key figures of the Indian resistance to her Paris flat. Meanwhile, she supported the Boers in every way possible, though some alternatives were more extreme than others. In December 1899 she went to Brussels to meet with the Boer diplomat W. J. Leyds, who represented the South African Republic. He was trying to use South African gold to coordinate support for the Boers throughout Europe. Maud horrified Leyds by suggesting that bombs disguised as lumps of coal be hidden in the holds of British ships filled with troops heading to South Africa. That meant young recruits, Irish as well as British, would die.

Maud told Leyds that Dr. Mark Ryan, the founder of the Amnesty Association, had approved this mad scheme, but she was wrong. Ryan, to the contrary, had warned Leyds against informing the wild Maud of their plans. Dr. Leyds objected, "But that is not a recognised means of warfare." Maud argued with him and said, "Why not?"

> Whether you kill your enemies on land or at sea, it does not seem to me to make any difference. And are evictions and concentration camps, which mean killing women and children, recognised forms of warfare? They are being used by the British Empire against both our countries.

Leyds told Maud that such a plot would turn the Liberals in Parliament against them, so it was out of the question. When it came to fighting England, Maud was in dead earnest. In other ways she could appear quite playful. For instance, she loved playing games, both with the press and with the men who followed her movements in Ireland on behalf of the British government. Of the two strong men who kept watch on Nassau Street in Dublin, where she had rented rooms above a bookstore, she wrote: "The tricks we used to play on those unfortunate sleuths would fill a volume."

Her sense of humor was singular. For instance, she brought a canary with her to the United States on her speaking tour. At the Savoy Hotel in New York she hid the pet, Twee-Twee, from two reporters by slipping it under her chair. The bird was in a little cage, covered with black silk. She was giving an interview on the treatment of Irish political prisoners in Portland.

> Suddenly, in a clear thrilling note, Twee Twee joined his voice to mine. The reporters looked round. One said, "Sounds like a bird."

I said: "What is this delicious music? Is it some wonderful new American invention of making invisible music?"

"It must be a musical box in the room below. Sounds mount," said one of the reporters and he continued the interview . . .

I got through the whole tour without Twee-Twee being interviewed but it required some maneuvering.

Maud enjoyed "maneuvering." She would no doubt have made a good general. Her memoirs, filled with incidents such as the one with her pet canary, are colorful and discreet. They freely mix up dates and places and alter names. She calls the child her father's mistress gave birth to "Daphne" instead of her actual name. Lucien Millevoye is written about only in the context of their political alliance. Iseult is never revealed to be her daughter. So though Maud's memoir is filled with entertaining stories about herself and her famous compatriots, it isn't always accurate. She was a fabulous mythmaker and self-promoter in newspapers and magazines, all for the sake of Ireland. To get a fuller picture, one has to look at contemporary newspaper accounts and memoirs of other players in the Irish cultural renaissance, one of whom was Yeats, but he too rearranged the past to present a more polished, coherent picture to the world.

Despite Maud telling the mournful poet in Paris that she had "a horror and terror of physical love," she seemed to enjoy men's company, to bask in their attention and to ably manipulate them. Perhaps her expressed abhorrence of physical intimacy was a ruse invented in order to soothe Yeats's battered ego. When Maud perceived males to be brave men of action like her father, rather than poets and intellectuals, she seemed drawn to them.

She did notice, admire, and spend time with other charismatic and notable men, many of whom she met in her travels promoting Irish independence. Her memoir is peppered with accounts of men who admired her and even proposed. She described the Norwegian Arctic explorer Fridtjof Nansen, whom she met en route to the United States and was also doing a lecture tour, as "very good looking." Noticing she was seasick, Nansen had a steward fetch Maud a chair so she could sit next to him on the deck and breathe in the fresh air. He wanted Maud to accompany him below to see how emigrants traveled in steerage, but the captain would not permit it. Class distinctions in Victorian England were strictly maintained by custom, if not by law. Nansen, like Maud, was very concerned with the plight of the disenfranchised. His interest in the plight of millions of stateless refugees after World War I spurred him to set up the High Commission for Refugees, under the League of Nations, later renamed the Nansen International Office for Refugees. The organization won the Nobel Peace Prize in 1938.

It seemed as if Maud and the handsome explorer had much in common, but no romance bloomed. Why she rebuffed so many smart, attractive potential suitors remains mysterious. She never stopped to reflect on the men whose attentions she flicked away, as if with a fan. Her secret commitment to Millevoye and their love child may have been one reason. And she had ambivalent attitudes towards marriage. Very unusual for her class and her era, she didn't even consider marriage a possibility for herself until she was well into her thirties.

In 1900 the estimation of women's intelligence in Europe and in the United States was low. They were considered too emotional entirely lacking in the good judgement needed to vote. A woman speaking her mind on political subjects was an anomaly. However, Maud was up to the challenge of changing minds and hearts about the role of women in public life. She traveled to twelve cities on her US tour. The first stop was New York, where she told an overflowing crowd of four thousand people at the New York Academy of Music opera house that "the end of the British Empire is at hand." On January 6, 1900, the *Boston Herald* reported on her stop in that city:

"What she says about the Boers is no sort of consequence compared with the way she does up her hair."

She had more success elsewhere. The *Blackfoot News* of Blackfoot, Idaho featured a big story in their January 20 issue, calling her "a new Joan of Arc. Maud Gonne wants to lead a Boer Army. She is the daughter of a British officer, but believes that England's flag is red with the blood of poor peoples." It is notable that for this interview, Maud made no claim of being Irish. In the United States perhaps she could be truthful, unlike in Dublin. The paper includes a paragraph-long flattering description of her person, as if the reporter wanted to date her, rather than describe her visit:

> And as she spoke a painter might well have caught inspiration for a picture of some prophetess or of the veritable Joan of Arc. A brow crowned with a halo of golden hair; large eyes which are now filled with indignation, now bathed in tears of pity; a graceful, slender and supple figure; the gesture large and noble; the whole appearance stamped with a character of extreme elegance—such is Maud Gonne.

Clearly, Yeats was not the only man to consider her looks extraordinary.

On her US tour she raised $3,000, now roughly $91,000. Most of that money went to her friend Arthur Griffith for his weekly paper the *United Irishman*. She supported and wrote for the penny pro-nationalist review, as did other Irish notables of the day: Yeats, AE (the pseudonym of mystic George William Russell), George Moore, and Padraic Colum. The paper effusively covered Maud's nationalist activities, generating more publicity for her.

In March of 1900 Maud returned to Paris from her second US tour. She was temporarily stopped from activity by an intestinal illness which kept her in bed. The six-year-old Iseult was sick too, with influenza, a viral disease that rampaged around the world in the early twentieth century and killed millions. From her bed Maud wrote an incendiary article called "The Famine Queen," which first appeared in her four-page Parisian news sheet *L'Irelande Libre* and then, on April 7, 1900, in *United Irishman*.

> For Victoria in the decrepitude of her eighty-one years, to have decided after an absence of half a century to revisit the country she hates and whose inhabitants are the victims of the criminal policy of her reign, the survivors of sixty years of organised famine, the political necessity must have been terribly strong . . . England is in decadence. . . . She has hypnotized the world with the falsehood of her greatness; she has made great nations and small nations alike believe in her power.

The lord lieutenant of Ireland ordered Dublin police to confiscate all copies of this issue of the *United Irishman*. Maud was pleased, because that meant her words mattered to the British government. As soon as she and Iseult were well again, Maud traveled on to Dublin alone to stir up more protests regarding the visit.

In April the *Irish Figaro*, a Dublin society weekly that appealed to "lady readers," published an editorial by Ramsay Colles stating that Maud Gonne was not only a liar but a spy in the pay of the British government because she received an annual pension of £300 from the British government for her father's military service. Tempers ran high. Arthur Griffith stormed into the office of the *Irish Figaro* on Grafton Street and beat Colles hard enough with his South African stick that it broke. Maud Gonne not only wrote for the *United Irishman*, she helped support it financially, and Griffith was outraged by Colles's assertion that a lady on his staff, his patron and a contributing writer, was a liar.

Maud sued Colles for libel and won, recalling, "I bought a new hat for the occasion." In court, Maud stated that she was neither in the pay of the British government nor a spy. She further insisted she was Irish because her father was Irish "and proud of it."

"What part of Ireland was he from?" the counsel asked.

"I don't know where he was born," Maud replied.

This was a lie because she knew her father had been born in London, but remarkably she won her case. Colles apologized to Maud. John O'Leary, who sat next to Maud during the trial in a show of support, congratulated her on her victory.

On Easter Sunday 1900, Maud gathered with other young women in the office of the *United Irishman*. Its cofounder Willie Rooney was serving as acting editor while his friend Griffith was in jail for two weeks for the Colles beating. To thank Arthur for his outrage on behalf of Maud, the women decided to replace Griffith's South African stick with an Irish one, a blackthorn topped off with a silver ring. While the dozen or so women were together, Maud suggested they form a nationalist organization of their own. They chose "Daughters of Erin" for their name and Rooney translated it into Irish: Inghinidhe na hÉireann.

The young women were sisters and sweethearts of the men who belonged to the Celtic Literary Society, which put on popular evenings of Irish poetry and song. Influenced by the suffrage movement, these women were not content to sit on the sidelines as their men went ahead and made important political decisions without them. An added emphasis of the Daughters of Erin, as opposed to the Celtic Literary Society, their fraternal organization, was to educate children in Irish culture and to offer them free classes in Irish history, literature, and industry. Before that happened, the women planned and executed their first notable project: "the Patriotic Children's Treat."

Organized by these women with the help of their men, it was billed as a reward to the thousands of schoolchildren who refused to parade in Phoenix Park for a free breakfast welcoming Queen Victoria during her April visit. Authorities had rounded up several thousand children for the occasion. The turnout for Victoria was small compared to what these Irishwomen accomplished: thirty thousand. Anticipating the huge numbers of children who would participate in the Patriotic Children's Treat, the women organizers chose Clontarf Park in north Dublin as their venue to dispense treats. On Saturday, June 30, 1900, together with their men, who also volunteered their time, the women organized some thirty thousand children to walk through the streets of Dublin until they reached the park. Maud and other women who formed Daughters of Erin led the procession.

In the park, the children ate an estimated fifty thousand donated buns and another twenty tons of donated sweets, along with countless oranges and hams. Decades later, grown men and women would see Maud and come up to her on the street to tell her how being part of this memorable procession marked their childhoods. It must have been an amazing experience to be one of those schoolchildren cheered on by their enthusiastic families as they walked the streets of Dublin. Yeats wrote in his memoir:

> In a field ... and in the presence of a Priest of their Church,
> they swear to cherish towards England until the freedom
> of Ireland has been won, an undying enmity. How many
> of these children will carry bomb or rifle when a little
> under ... thirty?

Gonne, herself in favor of violence as means to an end, inspired thousands of children to feel the same way and shape their mature lives around patriotic beliefs acquired in childhood.

When Maud was in Dublin she happily gave children drama classes while her friend, the writer Ella Young, taught them Irish history, weaving in Irish myths and legends with acknowledged facts. Like the Patriotic Children's Treat, free lessons in Irish, history, drama, dance, and music made a lasting impression on the young recruits.

In the fall of 1900, Arthur Griffith and Willie Rooney formed Cumann na nGaedheal, the "Federation of the Gaels," to combine different Dublin-based nationalist groups. The Daughters of Erin, led by their first president, Maud Gonne, joined Cumann na nGaedheal. That was the first time in the new century that women were welcomed into a men's Irish nationalist organization. In 1903, Cumann na nGaedheal morphed into the political party Sinn Féin, "Ourselves Alone," a party that remains a force in Irish Republican politics today. Maud had made important progress for patriotic and politically-minded young Irish women, all the more remarkable because she was no longer backed by Millevoye.

As noted, Maud's relationship with Millevoye had hit the rocks. For her, the amorous break was in tandem with a political one. When she discovered that the young chanteuse who Millevoye admired at the Paris opera was the real author of an article he printed in *La Patrie*, she knew the alliance was over. Maud didn't blame the end of her affair with Lucien on a fifty-year-old man's lust for a younger woman engaged in theater and journalism much like herself. Instead she attributed it to a setup by Georges Clemenceau, and called it a "honey trap." It was Clemenceau, she believed, who introduced Millevoye to the attractive young singer in order to seduce him and change his politics.

Judging from her memoir, perhaps because their relationship had been precarious for many years, Maud didn't seem utterly ravaged by its end, though a whole chapter in her memoir is called:"End of the Alliance." The sad but resilient Maud plunged forward into her next project: producing propaganda to stop young Irishmen from enlisting in the British war against the Boers. Enlisting, she told young men, would make them cannon fodder for the Empire that oppressed them and their families.

After "the end of the alliance," as Maud entitled that chapter in her autobiography, she and Lucien continued to see each other because they shared a daughter. Lucien remained an occasional visitor. As chairman of the French Army's committee on aviation, he was able to secure Iseult a job as a secretary at the newly formed Aviation Committee of France. So they had Iseult in common even if their "alliance" had broken apart.

After their breakup they remained sufficiently amicable to go together to join the crowd of ten thousand welcoming Paul Kruger, the exiled president of the doomed South African Republic, upon his arrival at the Gare de Lyon in Paris on November 22, 1900. By then having rejected both Yeats and Millevoye as suitable partners, Maud was in the market for a new man. Her new cause, the Boer War, introduced her to Major John MacBride.

Chapter 9
A Brief Disastrous Marriage

At age thirty-five in 1901, Maud Gonne was at a crossroads. Despite international fame and fortune and being acknowledged an international beauty, Maud was alone. She was so overwhelmed by this reality that she overcame her aversion to marriage.

Since women weren't accepted into Irish nationalist groups, Maud had spent the last ten years working solo. She had made women nationalist and feminist friends in France, but until now she had no such colleagues in Ireland. The planning of the Patriotic Children's Treat and the creation of the Daughters of Erin, in 1900, marked the first time Maud was supported by other like-minded women in Ireland. These enthusiastic nationalist women were young, in their twenties, the rising generation, unencumbered by their parents' prejudices against women being active outside the home. While most Irishwomen of Maud's age seemed to have accepted that they could neither vote nor be members of nationalist groups, the new generation of young women had been influenced to think otherwise by the suffrage movement.

While most English-speaking women Maud knew had married in their teens or twenties, she was a single mother in her thirties; Iseult was Maud's responsibility, not Lucien's. Being a single parent must have been difficult a hundred and twenty years ago. Today it has become more socially acceptable, but in 1900 Ireland the Catholic Church's response to the parents of children born out of wedlock was punitive. Maud left no record of the particular lonely struggle she had in being a single parent.

Another problem for Maud was that she was felled by time. No one, in either the Victorian era or our own merciless contemporary culture, is immune to the effects of aging. For the first time in Western culture, a number of aging women are visible as political leaders. In the Victorian era, apart from the Queen herself, the women's movement was literally constrained through the corset, and intellectually and politically limited in other ways. Women were not considered the equals of men in science, brain power, or judgement. Apart from the Queen, most Englishwomen had neither political nor economic power. Maud, by virtue of her independent fortune, was unusual in many respects, but that didn't immunize her from male expectations.

Yeats, despite his irregular poet's life, liked women to be beautiful. At a London dinner with Maud and Kathleen, he noticed that Kathleen had rested and looked lovely that night in her white evening gown. In contrast, Maud hadn't bothered to change. Exhausted, she dined in her practical dark traveling clothes. Kathleen explained her approach to beauty to Yeats, and he turned their conversation into the poem "Adam's Curse," where a "beautiful mild woman" says:

> To be born woman is to know—
> Although they do not talk of it at school—
> That we must labor to be beautiful.

Unlike Kathleen, Maud was no longer willing to labor to be beautiful. For a number of reasons, both personal and practical, she began to think seriously of marriage as a way both to end her loneliness and give Iseult a stepfather and the semblance of what was considered to be normal family life in twentieth-century Dublin. Living with Iseult in Dublin would have been impossible because of prevailing mores; if she had a child in her household, she also needed to have a husband. Otherwise, she would be shunned by the newspapermen, politicians, and poets with whom she fraternized.

For Maud, politics trumped love. Her approach to affairs of the heart meant uniting her political ambitions with a man's, as well as her body. It did not mean taking care of that man and being domestic, bringing him his breakfast or vice versa. She never received such daily nourishing attention from her parents, so it isn't surprising that a peaceful domestic partnership eluded her.

As if tailormade to fit Maud's specifications, Major John MacBride arrived triumphantly in Paris on November 6, 1900, where he was greeted by her and other members of the Young Ireland Society at the Gare de Lyon. He had famously routed the British in one of the battles of the Boer War with his Irish Transvaal Brigade, which would become better known as "MacBride's Brigade." His good friend Arthur Griffith introduced him to Maud and the other committee members.

At a Dublin men's club a few years before, British journalist Henry Nevinson had met Maud for the first time, and predicted a match for her with a man of action, not a wordsmith. "I saw the meaning of that strong and beautiful chin. I knew that her longing was for action in place of all the theorizing and talk, so general in Dublin . . . 'The first man of action,' I said to myself—'the first man of resolute action whom she meets will have her at his mercy.'"

Meanwhile Yeats, her unstoppable suitor, proposed for a third time. Maud turned him down with strong words: "You make beautiful poetry out of what you call your unhappiness and you are happy in that. Marriage would be such a dull affair. Poets should never marry. The world should thank me for not marrying you."

While her relationship with Yeats waxed and waned, at first her relationship with MacBride seemed to be one of mutual admiration and respect. For a brief interlude, they counted on one another.

In the winter of 1900, MacBride temporarily settled in Paris. He could not go home to County Mayo, his place of birth, because the Boers had awarded him South African citizenship. That made him an enemy of the British Empire, due to its refusal to recognize South

Africa as anything more than a colony. MacBride's options as an out-of-work war hero who didn't speak French were few. Plus, by 1901, the Boer War had tipped decisively in favor of the British; he no longer had the option of being a South African Boer military commander.

Britain poured 400,000 men into South Africa as reinforcements against the Boers and the Irish volunteers. Gold and diamonds had been discovered in the area, and Britain wanted to keep the land. In response, Maud encouraged Irishmen to volunteer to fight for the Boers like her new hero, John MacBride. However, by 1902 the superior forces of the British defeated the Boers; they kept their ownership of the South African gold and diamond mines.

In the winter of 1901 Maud and Arthur Griffith convinced the major to go on a speaking tour of the United States. MacBride had been hanging around in Paris with no job and no prospects. They thought he could successfully fundraise among the different Irish-American nationalist groups, rile up pro-Boer sentiment against the British, and help fund the two-year-old paper the *United Irishman*. At MacBride's request, Griffith and Maud wrote a lecture for him to deliver.

In America, the major found it awkward to stand on a stage in front of an audience and read from a script. The local papers reported he looked stiff and uncomfortable at the lectern. Maud records that MacBride wrote her asking to join him on his tour. She did so in February. With her coaching, he became more comfortable reciting a memorized speech. Once he gained confidence, she left him to finish the tour and returned to France to see Iseult, now seven.

She had been gone for close to four months. Maud was the second generation of motherless daughters in her family and, while raising her own daughter, apparently accepted upper-class customs. Even her beloved father had sent her and Kathleen to school in England for a year. In her memoir, Maud fails to mention that experience. As with other unpleasant or controversial information, she simply left it out. Without questioning these patterns, Maud repeated them.

She left Iseult for long stretches of a time at a Carmelite convent in Laval, France starting when the little girl was seven. Suzanne Koch-Foccart, the prioress, became Maud's friend and Iseult's godmother. Maud had a wide circle of friends and relations in France and in Ireland who began to play a significant role in Iseult's life as she grew up. As if in a play, various adults made recurring entrances and exits in Iseult's life as they passed through Paris or visited the family in Maud's summer home in Normandy. As Iseult grew into a girl, Maud spent more time with her. In 1902, Maud moved the eight-year-old from the convent in Laval to live together with her in Paris. Eileen, Maud's half sister who had been lodged with Maud's beloved nurse Bowie in Farnborough, England, also joined Maud's household that same year when Bowie died. In keeping with her nods to Victorian mores, Maud didn't reveal her real relationship with Eileen to other people including Yeats; in a letter to him she called sixteen-year-old Eileen the governess of Iseult.

During Maud's third lecture tour in the United States, MacBride marveled at the woman who could take all of what he described to his mother as "the knocking about." Presumably he meant the constant travel, the noise, and the crowds. According to Maud, he admired her ability to speak eloquently in public and her skill at writing rousing patriotic articles. The Irish major proposed.

After their acrimonious split, MacBride wrote that she had proposed to him first, through tears, telling him of her hard life. He claimed to think that by marrying her, "I was doing a good act for my country and for herself." Given her history of making the first move with men, this is plausible. Regardless of who initiated their marriage, Maud thought about the proposal for two years before she agreed, during which time she visited both his mother and brother in Westport.

Meanwhile, when MacBride finished his US lecture tour, he went back to Paris where he eked out a salary as assistant to the English-speaking correspondent of an American newspaper. He then had some means of support, but since his French was halting, his financial future in France was uncertain. As usual in her liaisons with men, Maud by virtue of her great fortune remained financially independent. It set her apart from the men she socialized with, but the difference between her income and MacBride's didn't seem to be a romantic disqualification.

As Maud mulled over whether or not to marry the major, her nearest and dearest advised against. She wrote her sister Kathleen: "Little sister, neither you nor anyone on earth quite knows the hard life I have led, for I never told of my troubles and I have preferred to be envied rather than pitied."

Despite the admiration her nationalist work earned her in Ireland, France, and the United States, Maud's life was difficult. Far from being the goddess praised by Yeats, she craved the human love and companionship of one man to whom she would matter more than anyone else. In her letter to her little sister, she admits that the mask she presents to the world is only that. Her inner reality is at odds with the picture of the tall, striking thirty-five-year-old independent woman she presented to the public.

She added another feather to her cap (an expression derived from native warriors adding feathers to their headdress for every enemy killed, which seems apt for Maud) acting in Lady Gregory's and Yeats's co-written play *Cathleen ni Houlihan* for three nights in Dublin in April 1902. Yeats wrote the part for Maud and was thrilled that she agreed to play it. The Irish National Dramatic Company put the play on, with the backing of the Daughters of Erin and the brothers William and Frank Fay who produced it. No one who saw the production could forget Maud playing an old woman, who transforms into a beauty who "had the walk of a queen," embodying Ireland for the audience as well as for Yeats.

Despite the accolades and publicity surrounding her comings and goings, her acting and her speeches, Maud seemed to have had the cavernous hole inside that the contemporary writer Hope Edelman attributes to motherless daughters, especially daughters who lose their mothers when very young, like Maud. Such women driven by their lack of a mother achieve to earn themselves attention and the sensation of being loved by the many, if not the few. Then they are able to express their deep emotions of loss. That is the reason Harvard-educated actress Rebecca Tilney gave for going into the profession: "I lost my mother when I was very young and it was a way to deal with that grief and express myself." Maud had great empathy for the evicted Irish tenants and emigrants who filled her packed speaking engagements. In a Victorian world of rigid social distinctions, Maud could be real with her emotions to an audience of sufferers, but from an entirely different largely economic cause.

Another issue of Maud's mid-thirties was that, as Iseult grew up, it was increasingly difficult to maintain the fiction that the adorable, appealing girl was her niece. Iseult left no written record of her childhood so we cannot know if this was confusing for her. How did Iseult reconcile the truth with the fiction? When she was living in the convent in Laval, what did Suzanne Koch-Foccart—the prioress and her godmother—tell her? What did the other nuns say?

In Paris, passing Iseult off as her niece was possible, given French social mores. That was one reason Maud had originally chosen to live in Paris. However, what was socially acceptable in Paris was impossible in Dublin due to the vise-like grip of the Irish Catholic Church and an increasingly puritanical Irish nationalist movement. As a young man, the way James Joyce dealt with Irish Catholic Dublin was to exile himself to continental Europe. Once out of his own country, he gained the necessary perspective to write his devastating portrait of the people he knew in *Dubliners* (1914). As for Maud, in order to have Iseult live with her in her new Dublin home, she felt the need for the legal scaffolding of marriage. As she bleakly explained to Kathleen:

> We are made that way that we need companionship and
> with Iseult growing up I cannot get this companionship
> outside marriage. Marriage I consider abominable but for
> the sake of Iseult, I make that sacrifice to convention. . . . I
> am getting old and oh so tired.

Another remarkable confession from Maud; her relentless life of
speeches, writing, protesting, and constant travel wore her down. As
photos show, she was no longer a blooming, statuesque soft-looking
young beauty. Instead Maud had a hard, determined stare. By 1900
the fullness her face had as a young debutante was gone.

Her fatigue must have stemmed from the intense schedule she
kept. Ironically, she took care of countless Irish nationalist men in
different ways, by paying lawyer's fees as she did for James Connolly,
or by financially supporting their efforts, such as Arthur Griffith's
nationalist newspaper. Maud brought one of the Treason Felony
prisoners, Jimmy Cunningham, to live with Bowie in England. Maud
boasted that Bowie "justified her Howth reputation as a healer, for in
a month, he was able to travel to America." In her constant whirlwind
of activity, who was there to take care of Maud? No one. Maud wrote
Kathleen in another letter:

> I think I will be happy with John. Our lives are exactly the
> same and he is so fond and thoughtful that it makes life
> very easy when he is there and besides we have a vitality
> and joy in life which I used to have once, but which the
> hard life I have had wore out of me, with him I seem to get
> it back again a little.

Maud never recorded how the major made life "very easy," but in
the happy delirium of their first meeting, MacBride and Maud and
Arthur Griffith stayed up all night talking in her Paris flat. Her first

few years of acquaintance with him must have been enjoyable, as she wrote to Kathleen:

> MacBride is a man I know *very* well. I have seen a great deal
> of him for the last two years and I know he is thoroughly
> sincere and honest. I can trust him entirely and think I will
> be happy. Of course he hasn't any money, but he earns his
> living as a journalist & I think we will always get on.

The major's mother and brother tried to dissuade him from the match. His mother, who had met Maud several times, did not think Maud would make him happy as a wife. His older brother Joseph who knew her from her three-day visit with him in Westport wrote: "She is accustomed to money and you have none, she is used to going her own way and listens to no one. These are not good qualities for a wife."

To top off the accumulating naysayers, her daughter sobbed when Maud told her the news and had to be dragged off by a nun. Iseult hated MacBride, and never seemed to get over it, and Maud failed in her attempt to win Iseult's support of MacBride as a stepfather. "I felt like crying too," Maud wrote. Why Iseult took a dislike to the major remains a mystery. Was she jealous of MacBride for earning her mother's attention when Maud was so often away? Did Iseult find him threatening? Did her reaction foreshadow her mother's allegations against MacBride one short year later, on Iseult's behalf? Iseult was not the only one distressed by her mother's upcoming marriage. Arthur Griffith strongly warned Maud in a letter:

> Queen, forgive me. John MacBride . . . is the best friend I
> ever had; you are the only woman friend I have. I only
> think of both your happiness. For your own sake and for
> the sake of Ireland . . . don't get married. I know you both,
> you so unconventional—a law to yourself; John so full of

conventions. You will not be happy for long. Forgive me,
but think while there is still time.

Despite the strong objections of family and friends, the couple
decided to go through with it and marry. Evidence suggests MacBride
drank more heavily after marriage. Maud, for all that she'd been
addicted to chloroform after her first child's death, never revealed
her feelings about the use of alcohol as an escape rather than the
fashionable drugs of her day. She is noticeably discreet on the subject
of Irishmen drinking except to say that she considered drunkenness
"a danger to the nationalist movement." John MacBride, from all
accounts, enjoyed going out to the pub with male friends, but before
their marriage Maud never mentioned his drinking in letters.

Maud had schooled herself to be brave from childhood, training
that enabled her to be impervious to cries of "stop" and "think," as
friends and family begged her to do, before taking action and forging
ahead. She refused to listen, even to her own dreams, and ignored
her father's warning when he appeared to her in a dream and said,
"Lambkin, don't do it!" Lambkin was his pet name for Maud.

To prepare for her marriage to John MacBride, Maud converted
to Catholicism. She was already sympathetic to the faith. It was the
religion of the majority of the rebellious Irish. Their English conquerors were Protestant. Descendents of the English army settlers
given land by the British crown were known as the Anglo-Irish
Ascendency. They were "ascendant" because until the twentieth
century they held most positions of power in Catholic Ireland. The
Penal laws keeping Catholics out of the professions, forbidding them
from owning their own land or a horse worth more than five pounds,
were enforced until the early nineteenth century. Maud who had
identified with the Irish country people since childhood had a good
impression of Catholicism. All the children she played with as a child
in Howth were Irish Catholic.

Grown, as a resident of Catholic France, she was favorably impressed by the practicioners of the religion. She trusted a convent and its head Suzanne Foccart enough to park little Iseult with her for several crucial childhood years. Maud and Suzanne Foccart became personal friends so much so that she and Iseult sometimes stayed at Foccart's home in Laval. Or Maud let Iseult stay with Foccart alone. Maud had also become friends with the Boulangist minister Canon Laval, whom she met in Royat more than a decade earlier. These two staunch French Catholics were part of Maud's inner circle, so they paved the way for her conversion to Catholicism.

The conversion would have fitted with her outlook: Catholicism was the religion of the majority of Ireland's population; it was the religion of the rebellious, ill-treated Irish. Maud must have thought that, besides allowing her to marry John MacBride, becoming a Catholic would make her a better nationalist. Just as important, she seemed to find in the Catholic religion a spiritual home that she had not found in the Anglican Church.

Explaining her conversion to Kathleen, Maud wrote: "I want to look at truth from the same side as the man I'm going to marry. The truth has many prisms and one can see it in different colors from the different sides one looks at it from." On some level, the mystery, theatrics and magic of the Catholic religion appealed to her, much as occult work with Willie had done. She had made the decision to board Iseult as a small child at a French Catholic convent. Other British-born Anglicans might have objected to their child being raised by nuns. Maud did not. As for their treatment of women, without irony she observed: "I'm afraid even the Church is inclined to treat the rights of women lightly." That was all she, the great fighter for women's right to be included in shaping Ireland's political destiny, wrote about the patriarchal structure of the Catholic Church. She had rebelled against the Irish nationalists' refusal to allow women into their societies, but never rebelled against the Catholic Church.

Maud never went on record objecting to the Irish Catholic Church's treatment of women except for that small aside in her autobiography. Ironically, right up until 1996, the Irish Catholic Church was notoriously hard on young unmarried women who became pregnant. That was when the last Irish Magdalene asylum, a Church-run laundry, closed. These laundries used unmarried pregnant women to do unpaid labor and forced them to give up their babies. The Magdalene laundries were named after the reformed prostitute Mary Magdalene of the Bible. In effect these new mothers, "fallen women," remained enslaved for an indefinite amount of time working off their room, board, and medical treatment. The only thing that separated Maud from one of those women cast out by their families and their communities was money and her intelligent choice of country to live in.

On February 17, 1903 Canon Dissard received Maud formally into the Catholic Church at Laval. For Maud, becoming Catholic seems to have been just another step in her artfully created construction of an Irish nationalist identity.

She completed her transformation on February 21, 1903 when she married John MacBride, first at the English consulate, then at her parish church in Paris. Lady Gregory, tired of Yeats running himself ragged after the elusive Maud, was in favor of the marriage. She was probably the only one besides the canon who applauded the match. She even gave Maud practical advice. She told her to marry in the English consulate in Paris or her fortune, by French law, would become her husband's.

From the beginning, the marriage had a strong political overtone. The wedding was reported by the *United Irishman* on February 28, 1903. The bride wore an "electric blue dress," and raised a glass to toast "the complete independence of Ireland." Her husband's best man carried a green flag to signify the Irish brigade that MacBride had led in South Africa. The Daughters of Erin sent their president, Maud, shamrocks and violets for the celebratory wedding breakfast.

Afraid to tell Yeats what she was going to do, Maud sent him a telegram. Her assurance that "I will keep my own name & to go on with all my work the same as ever," did nothing to quell Yeats's anguish. Yeats underestimated her desire to be part of the crowd. He wrote:

> Maud Gonne is about to pass away . . . you are going to marry one of the people . . . This (weakness?) which (thrust) down your soul to a lower order of faith is thrusting you down socially, is thrusting you down to the people . . . now I appeal . . . to come back to your self. To take up again the proud solitary haughty life which made (you) seem like one of the Gods.

If Maud didn't listen to her father's advice from beyond the grave, she certainly wasn't going to listen to Yeats.

The crazy political nature of Maud's marriage to the major was exemplified by the couple's honeymoon plan. On the last page of her memoir, Maud writes, we "started on our honeymoon from which we both thought there was great chance we would never return." Before she left, Maud had made her will, leaving her cousin May as guardian of her daughter Iseult, making this statement plausible.

What did her dire prediction mean? The newly married couple had chosen Spain for their honeymoon in order to assassinate the UK's new king, Edward VII. The royal couple's itinerary included a visit to Gibraltar, and that was where Maud and MacBride hoped to carry out the murder. The mission of the newlyweds didn't come to fruition for a number of reasons. On the appointed night, "MacBride went to meet his friends and carry out his mission, but came back drunk to their hotel room and would not say what happened. This was the final blow in a honeymoon that from the start had not been auspicious." The big plot fizzled out into the night air.

The next morning, Maud packed her bags and returned to Paris. MacBride went with her. In quick succession, she became pregnant and tired of MacBride's company. He reportedly spent most of his time, and much of the wedding sum she'd given him, out drinking with former army buddies in Paris. The money was under his own jurisdiction to spend as he chose and, to his credit, he saved enough to buy a Dublin property when he returned home. In a striking break with convention, Maud had financed her own dowry. As for the motives for MacBride's behavior, one can only speculate. He was unemployed, aimless, probably depressed by the defeat of the Boers.

Repeatedly, Maud left her busy Paris household for Dublin. Her hired help included a cook and her companion and editorial assistant, Mary Barry O'Delaney, who edited *L'Irlande Libre*. That meant her husband was the only man in a household of women and children. Maud relied on her good friend and fellow journalist, the feminist Avril de Sainte-Croix to supervise the household while she was gone.

In Dublin she pursued nationalist activities. In one protest she mobilized public opinion against the city of Dublin's welcome for Edward VII. From the window of her home, she hung a black petticoat on a broom handle. Instead of a black mourning flag, the petticoat signaled that the household was grieving over the visit. Festive Union Jacks decorated the homes of neighbors. The Dublin police force, run by the British, came to take away the black petticoat but Maud "was protected by a group of young hurlers with their sticks and the flag continued to fly bravely."

She kept up the pace of her activities. In October 1903, she walked out of the Irish National Theatre Society's production of J. M. Synge's new play *In the Shadow of the Glen*. She had helped Yeats, the Fay Brothers theatrical team, Lady Gregory, and various other patrons form the Society, but her ideas for the use of an Irish national theater differed radically from those of Yeats. He put art first, while Maud thought nationalist sentiment more important. As she wrote to him in a letter: "with me the National ideal is a religion and a Theatre Co unless it serves the National cause seems of little importance." Knowing its plot before she saw the play, Maud wrote Yeats: "From all I can hear, I think Synge's play is horrid." She also condemned the play in print.

Synge's offensive-to-Maud drama was an Irish riff on Henrik Ibsen's famous hit *A Doll's House*. Instead of a Norwegian woman slamming the door on her husband, *In the Shadow of the Glen* introduces us to a young Irish woman, deliberately named Nora after Ibsen's heroine. Synge's Nora is unhappily married to a skinflint of an old farmer who has just died that day. She confesses to a passing tramp that she only married the old man for his farm and money. The tramp asks her, as the newly independent lady of the house, if he can spend the night. She agrees. Meanwhile, her husband is only playing dead, in order to catch her with a young shepherd he knows she fancies. As soon as Nora brings the shepherd home, the husband pops up alive, shaking his stick. The shepherd, a gold digger himself who only wanted to marry Nora if she inherited the old man's gold, is spooked by the resurrection and takes off. The enraged farmer throws Nora out of the house along with the tramp. Without the economic safety her husband provided, the tough life of the road is Nora's future, which the tramp poetically asks her to share. Maud probably disliked the portrayal of a young Irish woman married to an older farmer, a not uncommon occurrence after the famine. She definitely thought it bad for the nationalist movement to show a young Irish wife cheating on her wealthy husband and rejoicing at his demise.

When Maud returned to her Paris flat in October 1904, the household was in an uproar. Her friend Mme. Avril and the women of her household claimed that her new husband, while drunk, had behaved indecently towards the females in the apartment, including seventeen-year-old Eileen Wilson, eight-year-old Iseult, Mary Barry O'Delaney (Maud's friend, companion and assistant editor of *L'Irelande Libre*), and the cook. Did he threaten them, molest them? Did he sexually molest Iseult? Or did he just stagger around drunk and disheveled in this household of women, behaving like an ex-soldier and scaring the women and children badly? No one knows the details, because Eileen refused to testify in court on Maud's behalf and Maud refused to allow Iseult to testify because of her age and the added issue of her illegitimacy. If it came out that Iseult was the love child of a prominent French political activist, that would have added another layer of scandal to the already sordid proceedings.

MacBride must have hoped they could work things out. In April 18, 1904, in the United States on a lecture tour, he told a *New York Evening World* interviewer, "While I cannot go to Ireland my wife can and she is over in Dublin now having our little Seagan christened. . . . I hope he will be the first president of our Irish Republic."

Or perhaps MacBride was playing the part of proud father for the adoring American press. Maud too had high hopes for their son Seán, as did Mary Barry O'Delaney. So much so that O'Delaney telegrammed the Pope in Rome in January 1904 when the boy was born: "The King of Ireland has been born."

Far from subsiding, the scandal about Maud and John MacBride's separation changed their lives. As usual, during times of trouble, Maud enlisted Yeats's support. As was his habit, he confided Maud's distressing story to Lady Gregory. It is impossible to know whether Maud's accusations were true. Iseult hated MacBride. Perhaps he had scared her before he moved in with them? Or perhaps she just hated him for no reason and was horrified at the thought of her mother's upcoming nuptials. Eileen Wilson, who had become acquainted with MacBride's brother Joseph, marrying him in August 1904, refused to testify against her brother-in-law in court.

Maud regretted allowing Eileen's name to be brought into the case. She wrote that Joseph MacBride "who lives in Westport is quite sober." Maud approved of Eileen's marriage to Joseph, even though she testified his brother was a licentious drunk. That Eileen refused to testify against him makes one question whether or not John MacBride had actually propositioned, let alone seduced, her. Like other famous divorce cases, Maud and MacBride's was peppered by acrimony and scandal, but evidence is inconclusive as to what actually happened.

The trial was ugly. In court, Maud brought witnesses to verify his drunkenness, and he brought witnesses in to prove that she was English not Irish, an insult to Irish nationalists. He believed her to be "only a weak imitation of a weak man," which reveals more about him and his ideas of proper male and female behavior in the Victorian age than it does her. To him, it was fine for a man to stray and satisfy his sexual needs, but women had no comparable rights to do so. Along with the Irish Catholic hierarchy, MacBride had ideas about proper gendered behavior. MacBride insisted he could not have molested Maud's friend and assistant Delaney because "she is downright ugly. Her looks would not tempt any man and her age is such to render such a suggestion preposterous. I would not be seen with her dead in a five-acre field."

According to the Irish Catholic code circa 1905, men could have relations with women outside the sacrament of marriage, but not women. Maud had told MacBride that she had relations with Millevoye before her marriage—a huge mistake. MacBride then claimed she had other lovers too. As an Irish Catholic male, he had trouble with the concept of a woman having sex outside the sanctity of marriage as it was against Catholic doctrine. He saw women as having to operate by different rules than men.

It took years to sort out the troubled couple's separation agreement and then it was to neither of their satisfaction. The point of contention was their son, Seán MacBride, born in January 1904. Each wanted custody. Maud had custody of her son by law in France. She was terrified MacBride would come steal the boy away and take him to Ireland, where her legal rights to custody were in question. In Catholic Ireland, divorce was not an option.

For an editorial titled "Why Marriages Fail," *Rockford Morning Star* interviewed Maud, "fresh from a Paris divorce court." The Illinois paper argued that "from the viewpoint of women's best happiness marriage was the best arrangement possible." Maud disagreed. "If a woman has really something worthwhile to do in the world, I say unhesitatingly that marriage is a deplorable step or is likely to prove so until after she has accomplished her work. If she is an ordinary commonplace woman, she might as well marry as not."

On the plus side, she had an intelligent, appealing son born out of the wreck of the marriage. Maud taught the little boy to speak French as his first language, so Seán and his father wouldn't be able to communicate. After MacBride moved back to Ireland, he sent the boy postcards. From the point of view of the child, it must have been confusing to have little contact with his father. That was Maud's wish. She worried about MacBride's drinking and wrote to his solicitor, Barry O'Brien: "If John keeps from drink and does not otherwise annoy me, I am not selfish and would gladly increase the opportunities for him to see the child, but it must be left to my discretion."

The separation between these two giants of the movement caused a split among Irish nationalists. They took sides. John O'Leary, who had sat next to Maud during her libel trial in Dublin, was for John MacBride, as was Arthur Griffith, who had broken his walking stick coming to the defense of her reputation. Those defections must have hurt. When in 1906 she went with Yeats to the newly named Abbey Theatre, the last and enduring incarnation of the Irish National Theatre, she was hissed at by members of the audience who called out "Up MacBride!" Counter-hissing rose up in support of Maud.

In 1905 Maud was prevented from running for vice president of the Daughters of Erin, despite having been one of the founders of the organization and its first president in 1900. The Daughters of Erin had joined Cumann na nGaedheal (Federation of Gaels), and MacBride had effectively eliminated Gonne from the running by pointing out that only people of Irish descent could be members. Maud, he told everyone in their joint circle, was English. Maud, to her dismay, had to prove Irish ancestry to nationalist satisfaction before she could be considered a candidate. Evidently, John MacBride won, because Cumann na nGaedheal did not accept her proof. That meant Maud could no longer be part of an organization she had been instrumental in creating. This was a great blow. In November 1905 she wrote to Yeats:

> My dear Willie:
>
> I hate to trouble you, but I want your advice and help. . . . Could you get Mr. O'Leary to write a letter which could be published saying he is satisfied as to my Irish descent and saying that the ruling of Mr. P. T. Daly at the Samhain convention [Cuman na nGaedheal's autumn Festival] was wrong?
>
> This thing pained me so much that I distrust my own judgement in the matter—I have worked with & for these people for nearly 20 years, I have sacrificed riches & position for this work & they say I am not Irish—It is bewildering & very saddening.

Her entire adult life had been spent working for the cause. If she didn't want to create more schisms within the nationalist movement, she had no choice but to back off. Her plea to John O'Leary through Yeats was futile. O'Leary backed MacBride against her, underlining the continued patriarchal nature of the Irish nationalist movement.

With O'Leary, Maud was up against the nationalist propaganda machine, the same machine that provoked walkouts (including by Maud) at Synge's *In the Shadow of the Glen* and riots at performances of *The Playboy of the Western World*. The nationalists objected to an Irish woman being shown as a cheater in the former, and an Irishman as a murderer of his father in the latter. Nationalist gossip tarred Maud as a fallen woman, a woman who was English not Irish. Such Irish nationalists found her unworthy of being married to MacBride. In January 1905 she wrote Yeats:

My dear friend

> I'm glad you know all. Thank you for your letter & thank
> you for all the trouble you are taking for me. . . . Your kind
> letters are a great comfort & I thank you for your generous
> sympathy—but Willie I don't want you to get mixed up in
> this horrible affair. By my marriage I brought this trouble
> on myself, and as far as I can I want to fight it alone.

Maud, the captain's daughter, wanted to be brave and face her enemies on her own.

As we shall see, she altered her stance when the reality of her solitary position became apparent. Upon hearing of her acute distress, Yeats, ever the indefatigable friend, tried to help by finding her a good lawyer, which she needed. In Irish Catholic nationalist circles she was getting a bad name. MacBride, still seen as a hero by Irish nationalists such as O'Leary, vilified his ex-wife in pungent, searing language.

Luckily, Maud was both resilient and resourceful. She found other things to do with her sudden free time, including focusing on the well-being of ten-year-old Iseult and baby Seán. She became a very involved mother, took up painting, and engaged in social justice work, once again on the world stage. Nothing could keep her out of the limelight for long.

MAJOR JOHN McBRIDE
(Born in Westport, May 7th, 1868).
Executed in **Kilmainham Prison, May 5th, 1916.**

Captain John MacBride, National Library of Ireland.

Maud, John MacBride, and baby Seán, courtesy of Iseult White.

Maud with Seán and Iseult, 1905, courtesy of Iseult White.

Maud Gonne in white, circa 1906, Reutlinger studio, Paris,
Bibliothèque Nationale de France.

W. B. Yeats, Lena Connell, 1910.

Iseult as a young woman, courtesy of Christina Bridgwater Rees.

Seán as a young man, courtesy of Iseult White.

Iseult Gonne at Laragh Castle.

Seán MacBride, 1948.

Maud in her garden at Roebuck House, courtesy of Iseult White.

Chapter 10
An Irish Son's Childhood in France

By 1905, Maud, then in her late thirties, could explore other passions both emotional and professional, bringing new richness and complexity to her life. She lived in Paris, where she was able to study painting and drawing with acknowledged masters. She drew her children and after a few years of intense study illustrated her friend Ella Young's book of Irish folktales.

Maude and MacBride legally separated in 1908. The court ruled there was evidence of drunkenness by MacBride but not sexual assault. Despite the separation ruling, Maud was not granted a divorce in France because she was not a French citizen but an English one. MacBride was granted visiting privileges which Maud subverted. The father and son rarely saw one another: he now lived in Ireland and they literally didn't speak the same language. When Seán eventually learned English, he spoke with a French accent. After the French separation agreement was reached in 1908, Maud relinquished her cherished idea of living in Ireland. She resigned herself to raising her Irish son in France.

The family spent more time at the summer home on the beach she purchased in Normandy in 1903, which she named Les Mouettes, or "The Seagulls." With extended family, friends, servants, and pets, Maud spent many summers and school holidays there.

Unfortunately, for much of the decade, the divorce case and bitter custody battle remained uppermost on Maud's mind, but it brought her close to Yeats in a new way. When he discussed her marriage with Lady Gregory, he told his sympathetic, tireless confidante that Maud confessed to him in London, a month after her disastrous honeymoon, that she married MacBride on an impulse of anger following her break with Millevoye and realized her mistake. Yeats wrote Lady Gregory: "I feel somehow that the Maud Gonne I have known so long has passed away; I had a feeling that a time of bitterness & perhaps of self-distrust & of fading life had begun for her."

Putting his turmoil at her marriage behind him, Yeats sprang into action once again as her protector. Maud had told her husband that Millevoye, whom MacBride had met at pro-Boer celebrations with her in Paris, had been her lover and fathered two of her children. Once MacBride knew she'd had one lover, he jumped to the conclusion that Yeats and the other men in her social, political, and cultural circles were her lovers too. He thought his attractive, charismatic wife cast a wide net, ensnaring many men besides himself.

MacBride is commonly alleged to have been intimate in South Africa with a Malay woman, by whom he fathered a child. The alleged mother of his child was descended from Malay slaves brought by the Dutch to South Africa from what's now Indonesia. Neither family, the MacBrides in Ireland nor the MacBrides in South Africa, has verified the connection, though it has become fodder for South African and Irish newspapers. Given MacBride's attitude towards sex outside marriage for men, it seems quite possible that he fathered a child while living in South Africa.

During the five years John MacBride and Maud Gonne's case dragged on and wound its way through the courts, Maud kept in constant touch with Yeats, reporting its excruciating progress. He wrote to her about the newly formed Abbey Theatre, and they discussed the many details of their complicated lives. To distract herself, Maud threw herself into drawing and painting. In July 1905, she wrote Yeats, "I'm working at painting all day long & trying to forget there is such thing as divorce suit on the 26th." That was when she heard MacBride's response to her lawyer's filing for divorce. MacBride denied all criminal charges and asked for separation. Through his lawyer, he refused to consider divorce as an option.

Throughout this long ordeal, Maud kept herself busy drawing. She did some lovely pencil drawings of her children, including one of Iseult, which she gave to Yeats. They continued to differ about the role of art and theater in Irish politics. Maud remained the agenda-driven Irish theater fan and subordinated her sophisticated love of good drama to her belief in the importance of having the correct political agenda for an Irish nationalist audience. Yeats, in contrast, placed art above politics. The two old friends amicably agreed to disagree on the role of theater in Ireland.

With a new party in power in Britain, MacBride was able to move back to Ireland in 1906. The Liberals, unlike the Conservatives, whom they ousted in a landslide victory, forgave the Irish who had fought against them in the Boer War. Since he was now in Ireland, MacBride posed no immediate threat to his French-speaking son in Paris. Maud had thought he would try to steal her son. He didn't. However, by the mores of Catholic Ireland, where he had reestablished residence, he could sue for custody of the boy, parade Maud Gonne's illicit affairs through the courts, and probably win. He could not sue for custody in France. Maud had won that battle.

By 1906, Yeats was no longer an inexperienced virgin. He'd had two love affairs and in 1908 was about to embark on a third, with Mabel Dickinson, a thirty-three-year-old masseuse, exercise teacher, and occasional actress at the Abbey. She was from the same Anglo-Irish middle-class background as Yeats. Their on-again, off-again liaison lasted until 1913, but he kept it secret from his friends. The relationship foundered when she claimed to be pregnant and pressed for marriage. It is difficult to know if being a masseuse in Mabel Dickinson's era had a sexual connotation. Did she have sex with her clients? Unknown. However, Dickinson eventually married a barrister, and the couple moved to England, so her reputation had not been ruined by her intermittent affair with Yeats. Perhaps Yeats's experiences with women emboldened him to be more sexually forward with Maud. Dealing with the thirty-one-year-old virgin a decade earlier, Olivia Shakespear had made the first move by giving Yeats his first-ever kiss on the mouth. Likewise, in 1898, Maud kissed him for the first time on the mouth. Much had changed since then for both of them.

By 1908 the poet was forty-three, a noted figure in international literary circles and relatively experienced as a lover, at least compared to his painful virginal twenties. While his star was rising as a literary and theatrical figure in the English-speaking world, Maud's stature was declining in France. As a nation, France increasingly rejected the demonization of England and made it official in 1904, when the two countries entered into the Entente Cordiale, or cordial understanding, settling their colonial differences in Africa and improving relations. Both nations buried their centuries of rivalry because of their common fear of the strength of a unified, formidably armed Germany. Maud's vilification of the British was no longer in step with the zeitgeist of French politics, nor did she have Millevoye to back her up through his connections in French media and political circles. She was at sea on many different levels and proved herself willing to try things she had never previously considered.

During the terrible upheaval of her divorce, Yeats found Maud much more loving and pliant. Throughout 1908 they wrote letters to each other, regularly communicating their "astral" experiences. Out of desire, they sent themselves back and forth to visit one another spiritually, even when they weren't in the same city. That year they renewed their spiritual marriage, a term Maud coined more than a decade earlier for their unusual relationship, based on her vivid dream of their being brother and sister sold into slavery in the desert by an evil master.

Yeats had a more conventional coupling in mind. He consulted French and English horoscopes for him and for Maud. The timing seemed auspicious for an actual union in the flesh. It is the consensus of scholars that in 1908, almost twenty years after their first tumultuous meeting, the two had sexual intercourse. We don't know if they had sex repeatedly or just once. Maud retreated from their newfound intimacy quickly, writing Yeats from Paris in December 1908, a day after leaving him:

> Dearest:
>
> It was hard leaving you yesterday, but I knew it would be just as hard today if I had waited. Life is so good when we are together & we are together so little!
>
> I have prayed so hard to have all earthly desire taken from my love for you & dearest, loving you as I do, I have prayed & I am praying still that the bodily desire for me may be taken from you too.

Why Maud preferred a spiritual rather than physical love remains a mystery. She had told Yeats that she had "a horror and terror of physical love," but by this time she had three children with two different men and had presumably mastered her terror. Or perhaps childbirth was such a painful experience before the invention and use of modern painkillers that she only associated sex with the arduous ordeal of giving birth. Although new medicine and new habits of sterilization would be introduced in the 1930s, increasing the chances of both mother and child surviving, childbirth in Maud's time was easily the most dangerous, painful event of a woman's life. All of these were taboo Victorian topics of conversation.

Maud could have shared one of the common, gendered Victorian ideas of her age: that women who believed Catholic dogma shouldn't take pleasure in sex and should only engage in it for the holy purposes of procreation. Or perhaps she was letting Yeats down gently, lying because despite her profound and enduring affection for this brilliant, loyal man, he wasn't attractive to her. Perhaps he was a lousy lover, inexperienced as to how to please a woman in bed. In his memoirs he records that during his first affair with Olivia Shakespear, he suffered from impotence due to nervous excitement. Maybe he suffered from impotence with Maud too. The nervous excitement must have been even greater.

Or perhaps the reality of having sex with his forty-two-year-old muse couldn't match decades of fantasies. Or hers about him. As was typical, Yeats would turn their experience into a poem, "His Memories."

> My arms are like the twisted thorn
> And yet there beauty lay;
>
> The first of all the tribe lay there
> And did such pleasure take—
> She who had brought great Hector down
> And put all Troy to wreck—
> That she cried into this ear,
> 'Strike me if I shriek.'

It certainly doesn't sound as if Yeats was able to pleasure her in any conventional sexual sense, though in a rough draft of his poem "Reconciliation" he wrote: "We've so remade the world ... the world's alive again." For him, this brief amatory success was to be celebrated. However, his attempts to persuade Maud to repeat the experience were rebuffed. Since her era was so much more discreet than ours, we don't know why. We don't know if sex after menopause was painful for her. Nor do we know if she ever enjoyed sex. We do know that she argued with Yeats by letter that "Michael Angelo denied the power of sex, *for a year* while he was painting the marvel of the Sistine Chapel." She seemed hoping to persuade Yeats to be celibate and conserve his energy for his haunting poems. If Yeats had been trying to convince her that ongoing sex—sex with her—was necessary for the full flowering of his poetic genius dealing with the great cause of Irish freedom, he failed.

By this time, unlike when he first met her as a poor young poet in London counting every farthing, he had many resources. He was a successful theater manager and poet, a cultural leader in Ireland. In 1908 Yeats had other women he could turn to for sexual and emotional intimacy. He was no longer starved of either by the changeable and challenging Maud. Her deepest most enduring love belonged not to him, but to Mother Ireland and her two children.

In 1908 she continued to fill her time with painting, and the care of Iseult, now fourteen, and Seán, five. Typically, during the Paris floods in January 1910, Maud helped rescue stranded Parisians and formed committees to feed and clothe them:

> "It really seems as if half of Paris is crumbling . . . All my time is taken up with relief committees trying to provide clothing & shelter for the hundreds of unfortunate people who have lost everything. I have lodged four in my own house & we have a great dortoir [dormitory] in the stables of the Passy marketplace where we feed & clothe hundreds & give shelter to as many as our limited space allows, & Passy is one of the least affected quarters in Paris. It is all a horrible nightmare." She sent her children out of town, to Les Mouettes, for safety from the chaos, accompanied by Mme. Dangien who looked after them while Maud immersed herself in relief work.

Then when Paris had recovered from the flooding of not one, but three of its rivers, Maud began a campaign to feed Irish schoolchildren. While exiled from Irish politics, it became her new all-consuming cause. A deliberate shift in focus for Maud, it was something she could accomplish without creating controversy among Irish nationalists.

Compulsory education had only been introduced in the late 1870s to England and Ireland. In 1906 the British Parliament passed an act that required local authorities provide children with free lunches during school, with the local community shouldering the cost. The Education (Provision of Meals) Act applied only to England and Scotland. Maud sensibly argued that if children were forced to be in school all day they needed something nutritious to eat to keep them in good health and able to learn. No one but Maud seemed to have thought to extend the 1906 act to Ireland.

Maud led by example. She organized a group of women, many from Daughters of Erin, to help prepare and serve food. The first food canteen she set up was at a Dublin parish where she knew the canon from his work on the Patriotic Children's Treat. Together with her women friends, she organized and fed 250 school children a pint of stew at lunch every day the first year. The next year, they doubled the number.

Along with the suffragist and nationalist Hanna Sheehy-Skeffington, Maud formed a women's committee to address the children's hunger. The women were aided in their work by Maud's old friend James Connolly. Through the Irish Trades Council, of which he was a member, Connolly drummed up trade union support from men. Picking up her pen, Maud wrote eloquently in "The Children Must Be Fed" in *Bean na hÉirann*, the monthly newspaper published by Daughters of Erin, in May 1910: "Few Irish people can have fully realised the cruel injustice inflicted on the children of the very poor, who are made to work without being properly fed . . . To let a child work unfed is crime."

However, there was a cost to her activism. Iseult and Seán were upset that Maud left them in February 1911 for the sake of "the hungry schoolchildren." Her seven-year-old and seventeen-year-old stayed behind in Paris with their caretakers while she organized a second canteen in Dublin. During her winter interlude in Dublin,

Maud attended to the physical wants of other children while her own, though well-fed, longed for the presence of their mother.

A good soldier like her father, Maud kept at the war she was waging: the battle against hunger in Dublin slums. She thought that Irish children should be rewarded for their hard work in school and that the British government and its Irish administrators should offer free lunches "to keep up the strength of the race." At the time, Dublin had the highest infant mortality rate in Great Britain, fifty percent higher than London. Through her connections, Maud finagled a private mass with Pope Pius X when she and Seán were in Rome. Maud hoped to enlist the pope in her fight to give free school lunches to Dublin children. She wanted him to support her work and quash the resistance she encountered from local Irish Roman Catholic clergy; instead, the pope said nothing about endorsing the program and gave Seán the communion wafer and a holy medal.

Hanna Sheehy-Skeffington, by now a good friend of Maud's, drafted a parliamentary bill to extend the school lunch act to Ireland. Maud presented that new bill to an MP in London. Eventually, through eight years of campaigning, the efforts of Maud and her colleagues paid off: thanks in large part to their work, the 1906 Education (Provision of Meals) Act was finally extended to Ireland in 1914.

Yeats, now in his forties and no longer content to pine abstemiously for his great love, continued his assignations with the attractive Mabel Dickinson. He corresponded with her at the same time as Maud. Maud wrote him from Les Mouettes on October 29, 1910:

Dear Friend:

I like the poems so much, even more than when I first heard them, the slight alterations you have made are improvements I think. Iseult read them & is wild over the music of the rhythm in them. There is a danger of my growing very vain when I think of these beautiful things created for me. Thank you.

Of all my work & all my effort little will remain because I worked on the ray of hate, I think & the demons of hate which possessed me are not eternal. What you have written for me will live because our love has always been high & pure. You have loved generously and unselfishly as few men have loved. It is what remains to me out of the wreck of life . . .

On a lighter note, Maud took Yeats, on one of his many trips to Paris, and her friend Ella Young to Rodin's Paris studio in December 1908. It seems remarkable that despite her social justice activities, Maud could be up to the moment in Parisian artistic circles. Rodin was then the most famous and successful sculptor in France, eventually honored by the construction of an entire Paris museum devoted to his evocative sculptures. Though Maud thought Irish art should promote Irish nationalist politics, she seemed to have no such demands for French art to serve the French republican cause. Although predictably, she preferred Italian renaissance painters and sculptures to Rodin's erotic sculptures of nudes.

Maud began to entertain again, hosting seminal leaders in the Indian independence movement like Bhikaiji Cama (aka Madame Cama) and Jawaharlal Nehru. She found common cause with Indian nationalists attempting to fight the Britain Empire and become a new nation. This was significant to the British men assigned to track Maud's Paris movements, including whom she socialized with. To the British leaders in London, this was further cause for alarm. It meant Maud was sponsoring not just Irish nationalists, but Indian ones, who were hatching an Indian revolt.

Yeats met Iseult in Paris in 1905. It was the first time he'd seen her since she was five. He was charmed by the eleven-year-old girl who had the look of her mother in three-quarters profile. The three of them went to the Louvre. Summers were spent with the children at her seaside home in Normandy. Friends and relatives, including Yeats, a frequent visitor, enlivened the children's holidays. Maud took great pleasure in showing Yeats the nearby marvel of Mont-Saint-Michel, a tidal island off the Normandy coast, with its majestic stone monastery and fortress walls. During many visits, Yeats observed Iseult grow into a sophisticated, well-read teenager. He wrote "To a Child Dancing in the Wind," after seeing her dance on the Normandy beach. Every summer for much of the next decade (1905–1916) Yeats visited Maud's eclectic household. Yeats taught young Seán to fly a kite on the beach.

Unable to be idle, when World War I broke out in 1914, Maud, forty-seven, and Iseult, now twenty, nursed soldiers in the Pyrenees.

Maud and Iseult were appointed lieutenants, which gave them the right to travel with the army as nurses. Three months of Red Cross nursing left Maud exhausted, despairing at "patching up poor mangled wounded creatures in order that they may be sent back again to the slaughter." She expressed similar thoughts to Yeats, saying "I would like to go & stir my hungry children's potato pot a little [return to her work with Dublin schoolchildren]. I feel it would be more useful work for me than to go on nursing soldiers patching them up in order that they may be sent back again, to be gored again . . . I have no military enthusiasm & can see nothing but misery in this present war."

After another immersion in six months hard nursing in Paris-Plage, a small seaside town in northern France popularly known as Le Touquet, Maud wrote: "within sound of the cannon . . . I am rather worn out & had to take a rest. All I want to do now is to work for peace. It is the only thing worth working for. How to begin? I don't know. I feel so bewildered and helpless."

Maud's experience nursing the first generation of men to suffer the devastating weapons of modern war—mustard gas, fast powerful machine guns, bombs dropped from airplanes—had a lasting impact. John Quinn, the Irish-American lawyer who had become her friend and advocate during her divorce trial, had been in favor of the United States entering the war, which she found strange. She wrote him, "You I believe, still see beauty in war, I did once but hospital and broken hearts & the devastation & destruction of all art and beauty have changed me and I bow to any peace advocate. They are the real ones who are showing Moral Courage." No doubt her excruciating experience nursing men in World War I caused her to become an admirer two decades later of Gandhi, who achieved remarkable results by leading massive nonviolent protests against British imperial rule in India.

While Maud remained in France, Irish nationalist hopes began to coalesce around the passage of the Home Rule Act being debated in Parliament. Three decades after Parnell's death, it seemed possible this legislative solution to Ireland's problem might work. Ireland could remain part of the British Empire yet have its own independent parliament. Ulster Unionists vehemently protested the bill as did conservative MPs in Parliament. Northern primarily Protestant Irish were hostile to the idea of being subject to the parliamentary rule of the Catholic Irish majority in the south. Although the Home Rule Act was finally passed by Parliament in September 1914, excluding six northern counties, including Ulster, it was immediately suspended on account of the outbreak of World War I. Parnell's vision of a Parliamentary solution to Ireland's problems evaporated.

Meanwhile Maud kept her cherished dream of a republican Ireland alive. It was the persistence of this dream that enabled her to admire her estranged husband's sacrifice of his life for the Irish republican cause. On April 24, 1916, he wandered into the middle of the six-day Easter Rising in Dublin and became part of it. Her old friend James Connolly, whom she had once bailed out of jail and fed breakfast, was one of the instigators. The armed men, helped by some two hundred women belonging to Cumann na mBan, seized key Dublin locations and proclaimed an Irish Republic. Promised

German weapons failed to appear. Increasing the confusion, Irish volunteers, under orders from another nationalist leader, Eóin MacNeill, refused to take part. Meanwhile, the British poured in much greater numbers of troops with superior weapons to put down the insurrection. The English outnumbered the Irish urban guerillas twenty to one, crushed the rebellion, and placed Ireland under martial law. Upwards of thirty-four hundred Irish men and seventy-nine women were arrested and interned. Many were ignorant of the rising, so more than half were released within two weeks.

The seventeen men blamed for the Easter Rising, who had signed the Proclamation of the Republic, were swiftly tried and executed by court martial. They were not allowed lawyers or anyone other than themselves to speak in their defense. The men had to answer the charges against them from their court-appointed prosecutor. Mercy was in short supply. The badly wounded James Connolly was carried by stretcher to what was known as the Stone-Breakers' Yard in Kilmainham Gaol. Although he probably would have died soon enough from his injuries, English soldiers strapped him upright to a chair and shot him dead. John MacBride was among those sentenced to death. He refused to wear a blindfold and looked straight at the firing squad. Yeats immortalized MacBride as a "drunken vainglorious lout," in what is arguably one of his finest poems, "Easter, 1916."

> This other man I had dreamed
> A drunken, vainglorious lout.
> He had done most bitter wrong
> To some who are near my heart,
> Yet I number him in the song;
> He, too, has resigned his part
> In the casual comedy;
> He, too, has been changed in his turn,
> Transformed utterly:
> A terrible beauty is born.

Quinn described MacBride's death as "a fine one . . . the best end possible for MacBride, a better end than living in the past and drinking and talking out his life." Not just Maud's estranged husband, but her old friends including James Connolly were among the dead. That must have pained her terribly, but the Easter Rising enabled her to transform her life dramatically. Maud changed tack. Rather than continue to describe MacBride as a threatening, salacious monster who might kidnap Seán, she told their son that he could be proud of his father for dying for Ireland. If twelve-year-old Seán thought it peculiar for his dread father to become a hero, he kept it to himself.

He had only met his father a few times, and knew him mostly from postcards. Seán remembered learning the news of his father's execution while he was at school in Paris:

> The rector made a very eloquent speech and indeed I always
> felt gratitude towards him then, saying that my father had
> been executed by the British, who were allies of the French,
> but who had occupied Ireland and treated it as a colony,
> and the Irish people were fighting for their liberation . . .
> my father had been one of the Irish patriots that had risen
> against Britain and deserved their respect and prayers.

With MacBride's death, Maud felt that she could return to Ireland, which she considered her home, and she immediately planned to move back to Dublin with her children. It had taken a self-imposed exile to explore other sides of her personality: her love of art, her long simmering connection with Yeats, and more importantly, to spend happy times at the beach with her children. In Dublin in 1918 she was able to transform herself again, this time into "the Widow MacBride."

Chapter 11
Rising Again: Easter Widowhood in Dublin

Women taking a role in politics as Maud had done—from her twenty-first year, in 1887, until her death in 1953—was highly unusual in early twentieth-century Europe and in the United States. In May 1916, when Maud's estranged husband was executed by firing squad under martial law, Irish women were six years away from getting the vote, American women three, and English women twelve. It is startling to realize that French women did not actually cast a vote until the first election held after their country was liberated by the Allies, on April 29, 1945. Seen in this context, Maud deserved her Irish nationalist moniker as "the Irish Joan of Arc." Despite the political disadvantage of her sex, she proved herself a remarkable leader of Irish men, women, and children.

After MacBride's death in 1916, Maud kept trying to win permission to return to Ireland. A close watch had been kept by the British on her movements for decades. They branded her a radical, dangerous Irish nationalist. Under 1914's Defence of the Realm Act, she was denied entry to Ireland. Though she had packed up her Paris household and her children in preparation for moving to Dublin in November 1916, the British War Office informed her they could only travel as far as England. Ireland remained forbidden to Maud. So, because she had given up her comfortable home in expectation of moving, she unpacked and rented a dingy, cramped apartment in Paris. Then she waited to hear from the War Office. 1916 dragged into

1917, and by the spring of that year the Gonne family had decamped to their Normandy home. Yeats, possibly out of habit, proposed to Maud—for a fourth time—asking that she promise first to give up politics, including her work with political prisoners begun decades earlier. Of course, as Yeats must have known she would, she refused him. Later that same summer, Yeats proposed to Iseult with whom he had become increasingly enamored. Unlike her mother, she was more interested in literature than politics. She was twenty-three to his fifty-two, and like her mother at that age, she was reputed to be a six-foot-tall beauty. Lady Gregory approved the choice of daughter over mother, because she considered Iseult much more conducive to Yeats's goal of forming a peaceful, creative artistic family.

Iseult thought it over for about a month before saying no. She worried that Yeats, who had become a constant in her life as well as her mother's, would take offense, claim she was being "selfish," and end their relationship. He did no such thing. Instead, he quickly adjusted and looked around for another young woman suitable for marriage and children. Past fifty, he was finally at a stage where he could afford to marry and father children. Playing a fatherly role to Maud's children, he demonstrated that he was capable of being a father for real.

Meanwhile, Maud had become impatient to get Seán into an Irish school at the start of the September school year. She wanted him to grow up in Ireland rather than France and, like his father, she wanted him to do great things for the country. Accompanied by Yeats and her two children, she took a ship on September 17, 1917 to Southampton, England, where she was stopped and physically searched by British officials. Yeats was helpless to prevent it. Again, officials warned Maud not to travel to Ireland. So instead the little party went up to London, where they stayed at Yeats's apartments in Woburn Walk while he lodged at the Arts Club, one of the many clubs to which he belonged.

Yeats had by now published many lauded books of poetry and celebrated plays, started Ireland's first successful national theater, toured and lectured in the United States, and had earned enough money to secure a loan and buy his first house: Ballylee Castle, formerly owned by his great friend Lady Gregory who had brought it to his attention and helped negotiate the deal. It was Yeats's hope to one day live in Ballylee with a family of his own.

Despite Iseult's refusal of his proposal, he continued to be of service to her. In London, he secured her a job editing *The Little Review* for the talented young Ezra Pound, Yeats's assistant of the previous three years. Pound was married to Dorothy Shakespear, the daughter of Yeats's first lover, Olivia Shakespear. Yeats had once again grown close to Olivia. Dorothy's best friend was a sophisticated lover of literature named Georgie Hyde Lees, of whom we will hear more later.

Pound's marriage did not prevent him, a budding fascist, from having an affair with his beautiful young assistant Iseult. Pound was engaged by the family to tutor Seán, but neither he nor Seán remembered the arrangement fondly. A smart thirteen-year-old, he probably knew his older sister and the married Pound were lovers. Seán had been raised Catholic, but was too discreet to mention Pound's dalliance with his sister in his memoir. The illicit affair no doubt complicated Pound's attempt to "jam Sean's very allergic head" with Ovid. Presumably Seán was allergic to Pound, not to Ovid.

While Iseult was carving out an independent existence in London, the restless Maud determined to go to Dublin. She never took Yeats's courting of Iseult seriously, and was correct in intuiting it would not result in an amorous relationship. In addition to Iseult, Yeats had over the previous few summers been smitten by the twenty-five-year-old Georgie Hyde Lees, who had assisted him in occult work. Less than a month after Iseult turned him down, he proposed to Lees. She accepted, and the fifty-two-year-old poet's lonesome shilling-counting journey through life ended.

Georgie Hyde Lees came from a wealthy family, so her fortune combined with Yeats's own earnings meant he never had to worry about money again. They married on October 17, 1917. Yeats finally fathered two children of his own with his young wife: Anne in 1918 and Michael in 1921.

Meanwhile, though under surveillance by British detectives from Scotland Yard, Maud kept her gaze fixed unswervingly on Dublin. She wanted to throw herself back into the nationalist mix and make up for lost time. The ever-elusive and intrepid Maud made a plan to evade the detectives. She enlisted thirteen-year-old Seán. He noted that while his mother went for a daily soak in a Turkish bath, the detectives passed the time at a nearby pub.

So, one January day, Maud entered the Turkish bath as her tall self, but came out disguised as a bent old woman, as if she were once again playing the part of Mother Ireland. She traveled to Dublin and arrived without incident. In Dublin, no one recognized her in disguise, not even her friend the suffragette and nationalist Helena Molony. As planned, Seán arrived separately from his mother in Dublin, where he stayed with Maud's Daughters of Erin friend Dr. Kathleen Lynn. Maud secured a house for them on St. Stephen's Green, the lovely park in central Dublin. The mother and son moved in and began to enjoy the cultural and political ferment of the city. George "AE" Russell, the writer and painter, a longtime friend of both Yeats and Maud, held a regular Monday night salon that Maud and Seán attended. That spring, Maud began giving political speeches again at rallies and protests.

Probably it was not a good idea for her to draw attention to herself politically, because on May 17 the police snatched her from the streets of Dublin. She and Seán were walking back from Russell's Monday night salon. The police took her to Bridewell prison. They had no warrant and didn't need one under the Defence of the Realm Act. Seán followed the van to Bridewell and returned with food for his mother and her warmest fur coat. The next day, Maud was transported to Holloway Prison in London, a women's prison that remained operational until 2016.

A little over a week after her arrest on May 25, the enterprising Seán followed his mother to London, where he stayed with Iseult. Instead of going to a local school he worked tirelessly for his mother's release, enlisting all their distinguished friends including Yeats and John Quinn to write letters to pressure the authorities. In his own letters to the Home Office, Seán begged to visit his mother, asserting he could not settle his schooling until he could discuss it with her in person. Finally on July 8, three months after she had first been detained, he was allowed into Holloway Prison. His mother, as he discovered, was kept in her cell twenty-three hours a day. Letter writing was limited to three and a half pages per week. That must have been difficult: she was such a good correspondent. The watchful eyes of prison guards made sure conversation was confined to the subject of schooling. The guards were under orders to escort Seán out immediately if talk turned to politics.

At the kind invitation of Yeats and his new wife, Seán spent the summer with them in Galway. They arranged his tutoring with a local schoolmaster. Throughout this peaceful interlude, Seán kept up his letter writing campaign to the Home Office. He reported that his fifty-two-year-old mother had lost about two stone, or thirty pounds, was plainly "very ill" and needed a doctor. He reminded them that Irish nationalist Thomas Ashe had gone on hunger strike in jail. As punishment, Ashe's boots, bed, and bedding were removed by the implacable prison authorities. Ashe was violently force-fed but died on September 25, 1917. Over thirty thousand people attended his Dublin funeral. Seán warned that his mother was liable to go on a hunger strike if not released, and who knew how many mourners would mass in her honor. The British wartime government did not need more bad publicity such as that generated by Ashe's death.

Prodded by Seán's letter, the Home Office agreed to let Dr. Tunnicliffe, a pulmonary specialist, examine Maud Gonne on October 22, 1918. The doctor advised she be released and receive "active medical and open-air treatment without delay," in order to halt her pulmonary illness, which he diagnosed as tuberculosis. Maud's notable friends in the United States and Ireland and members of the public, alerted to her sick, worn-down condition, pelted the authorities with letters begging for her release. On October 29, 1918, after five months in prison, Maud was delivered into the care of a London nursing home.

In late November, ignoring Home Office orders, she traveled to Dublin where she reunited with her son. Seán joined the Irish Republican Army the next year. Like his father, who had been a member of the Irish Republican Brotherhood as a teen, Seán was one of the younger members of the IRA. He kept his membership secret from his mother who naturally worried about his safety. During the tumultuous years preceding and following the founding of the Irish Republic in 1922, Maud continued her work for the humane treatment of political prisoners.

In 1922, Maud and Seán moved into Roebuck House, located in a Dublin suburb close to where Maud spent her early childhood. John MacBride had left the large Georgian brick house, its lodge, and garden to Maud and their son. Six years after his execution, his will was finally settled. Maud spent the rest of her life at Roebuck House with Seán, and later his wife and their two children and friends.

In 1926 Seán, twenty-three, married Catalina Bulfin, twenty-five, the daughter of a well-known journalist. Her nickname was "Kid" and her politics matched Seán's. Kid already knew Maud and Iseult, as the three women had been arrested and held together in Kilmainham Gaol, where the leaders of the Easter Rising had been executed. The Gonne-MacBride women were suspected of being part of the IRA's weeklong takeover in 1922 of the Four Courts building in Dublin, so called because it contained the four main courts of civilian government. It was a protest move by ardent nationalists against the British-engineered Anglo–Irish Treaty. The controversial treaty, which concluded the War of Independence, divided the small island of Ireland into two: the primarily Protestant north remained part of the United Kingdom and became known as Northern Ireland, and the largely Catholic south formed the new Irish Free State, later the Republic of Ireland. Ireland was independent of Britain for the first time in five centuries, but split. A civil war erupted immediately after the signing of the treaty.

Seán believed that, like her pacifist friend Hanna Sheehy-Skeffington, Maud had become reluctant to join any Irish political organization that promoted the use of force. Maud helped found the Women's Prisoner Defense League (WPDL) and became its secretary. The WPDL helped families find information about their incarcerated loved ones, what jail they were in for instance, so the detainees could have provisions such as blankets and nourishing food.

The Free State government banned the WPDL. In response, clever Maud and the other women running the organization changed its name, and for further security changed their designated meeting spots constantly to avoid government spies. During the bloody Civil War of 1922–23, Maud and her friend Charlotte Despard organized cottage industries at Roebuck House to give work to young republicans without jobs, while also setting up a makeshift hospital there to nurse wounded victims of the sectarian conflict. The new republican government proved as merciless as the former British government in imprisoning men and women who opposed its creation or held out hopes for a united republic. The same jails were used to detain these hardcore nationalists, only now the grim prisons throughout the Free State were administered by Irish personnel instead of British.

Tempered by experience and the ordeals of nursing, Maud became something of a pacifist, a radical change from her former views supporting the use of force and terrorism to achieve Irish independence. After great personal loss and years spent patching up the mangled men of World War I, Maud's thinking had shifted radically. In old age, she became an admirer of Mahatma Gandhi, so much so that in February 1948 she confided to her young journalist friend Ethel Mannin that Gandhi's 1948 assassination shook her so profoundly that she ceased letter-writing. That, she said, was why she had been so slow to respond to Ethel. Maud then was eighty-two. As she became increasingly infirm, her activities became more mental than physical. Her body had slowed down, but not her mind.

 Hearing about the terrible conditions in the republic's prisons must have reminded Maud of the men she visited in the fortress prison in Portland, off the west coast of England, decades earlier. The Irish Free State government of Éamon de Valera was arguably as cruel to its political prisoners as the hated British. In 1946 in Portlaoise Prision, political prisoners like Seán McCaughey were allowed out of solitary confinement once a week for a bath. They received no letters, no visits, never went into the open air and never felt the sun, profoundly damaging their physical and mental health.

In a letter to the *Irish Times* in 1946, Maud, then in her late seventies, forcefully declared: "Let no more young lives be sacrificed to uphold an old British prison rule of Victorian origin: be speedier than death in releasing young McCaughey." She was pleading for the release of other political prisoners; for McCaughey it was too late. While demanding special treatment as a prisoner of conscience, including the right to wear his own clothes and have visitors, McCaughey died on a hunger and thirst strike, May 11, 1946. He was thirty-one, just one of many Irish people to die miserably in the twentieth century during what was called "the Troubles."

During the inquest into Seán McCaughey's death, thirty-two-year-old Seán MacBride, former IRA chief of staff who had become a human rights lawyer, argued that the prison doctor would not have treated a dog the way McCaughey had been treated in jail by the guards. MacBride's searching, smart questions brought into public awareness the terrible conditions in maximum security prisons such as Portlaoise. The negative publicity helped improve the treatment of political prisoners in the Free State.

As adults, each of Maud's children embraced one of her lifelong passions: anti-Semitism or the human rights of political prisoners.

Both of Iseult Gonne's parents were anti-Semites, so it is not surprising that Iseult shared their negative, conspiracy-oriented opinion of Jews. Seán MacBride had a different father of course, and from an early age had been recruited into Irish nationalist intrigues by his mother.

Maud's anti-Semitism drove her wartime activities in the Republic of Ireland. As a practical measure, Maud chose Victor Gollancz, a Jewish man, as publisher of her 1938 memoir *A Servant of the Queen*. She wanted to make money from the sales of the book and believed that a Jewish publisher could do so. Her behavior, like that of the Irish government, was mixed. Even though detestation of the British seems to have been ingrained in much of the Irish population, the Irish government refused to ally itself with Nazi Germany against Britain. The Free State government, as it was then known, was committed to remaining neutral, and the Irish army's intelligence unit began surveillance on Maud.

Nevertheless, during the war Maud corresponded with Oscar Pfaus, a German spy who arrived in Ireland in 1939. In Ireland, Pfaus contacted the IRA and did his best to convince them to join the Germans against their common enemy, the British. Pfaus's exchanges with the IRA culminated in an act of sabotage in the United States: the 1940 explosion at a New Jersey armaments factory in which fifty-two were killed and another fifty injured. The IRA allegedly carried out the act at the behest of the Germans, although it wasn't clear if the explosion was accidental or a deliberate act of terror.

Though she herself never actually compromised Irish neutrality or did anything more than write letters to an identified German spy, Maud was part of an extended Irish network of Nazi sympathizers. She wasn't the only Irish nationalist to feel the way she did. On May 2, 1945, Éamon de Valera, then the Prime Minister of Ireland, went to the Germany embassy to offer his condolences on the death of Hitler. Maud made no comment on Hitler's suicide, but after the Second World War officially ended, she wrote letters as part of a campaign to spur the Irish to send food to Germans or take starving German children into their own homes. Although she lived in France for thirty-some years, she never publicly mentioned the orphaned French-Jewish children, nor the thousands and thousands of French-Jewish children murdered by the Nazis with the help of the French.

Iseult was very much her mother's daughter. Following her affair with the fascist sympathizer Ezra Pound, Iseult took up with an Irish nationalist who also proved to have an admiration for the German fascist movement: Francis Stuart. He was eight years younger, seventeen to her twenty-five. In January 1920 they ran off together to London. At Maud's insistence they formalized the relationship, returning to Dublin in April, where they were married—again at Maud's urging—under the auspices of the Catholic Church. Stuart was then a budding novelist, born to Irish parents in Australia. The marriage was rocky right from the start, though the couple went on to have three children. Their first child, Dolores, tragically died of meningitis, like Iseult's brother Georges. Maud tried to comfort her devastated daughter. Yeats attempted to broker a separation agreement between Iseult and Stuart early on in their marriage, but the agreement didn't hold, probably because Iseult was very attached to her husband.

After two decades, Francis left Iseult and their children to take a job lecturing at a university in Berlin, a post Iseult helped him obtain. It didn't occur to her that Francis's commitment to Nazi Germany would prove stronger than his commitment to their family, especially when he fell in love with one of his German students in Berlin. After his university post finished, he began to work in propaganda for the Nazi government.

In 1939 Francis broadcast in English out of a Berlin studio to reach an English-speaking audience and promote the Nazi cause. His broadcasts were specifically aimed at an Irish audience, but that didn't endear him to Maud or to Seán. Seán disliked Francis Stuart because of his treatment of Iseult. After Iseult died in 1954, Francis married his German sweetheart, Gertrude Meissner, and returned to Ireland. He had probably worried about a scene with Iseult and the impossibility of bringing a divorce case in Ireland; divorce was forbidden by the constitution until 1996. While Iseult was alive, he could not remarry. He wrote many novels— some acclaimed, some not—but didn't financially support his children. When his German wife died, Francis's son with Iseult, Ian Stuart, generously took his father in, saving him from living out his days in a Dublin nursing home. Francis spent the last final two years of his life in Laragh Castle, County Wicklow, the home which Maud had purchased for Iseult with proceeds from the sale of Les Mouettes.

In 1940, Iseult was in the news like her famous mother. She made the newspapers when she was arrested for harboring Captain Hermann Görtz, an associate of Nazi second-in-command Hermann Göring. Iseult, the avowed anti-Semite, had fallen in love with the German spy while sheltering him while her husband was in Berlin. The two had an affair. Refusing bail, Iseult was held in Mountjoy Prison for six weeks and then acquitted of all charges. Stephen Carroll Held, an IRA member with German heritage who had also aided Görtz, was convicted and sentenced to five years in prison. Iseult may have been acquitted because her husband was a notable player in the employ of Nazis in Berlin, and at the time it seemed as if the Nazis might win the war. There was also the matter of Iseult's famous mother—her prominent family may have saved her from a harsher sentence.

Iseult's children seemed to adore their mother. Her granddaughter Christina Bridgwater Rees and her cousin Anna MacBride White helped preserve her memory by editing a book of her letters to Ezra Pound and Yeats. Her son Ian Stuart became a notable twentieth century Irish sculptor, showing both in the Paris Biennale and at the Museum of Modern Art in New York. Ian sided with his father, who called Iseult the "real Nazi." Ian repeated this claim: "My father wasn't, she was. She'd have gone to bed with Hitler, given half a chance." Nevertheless Ian, who described himself as apolitical, loved his mother and looked after her until she died at the age of sixty, a year after Maud. It was ironic that Maud eluded the early death she had feared because of trouble in her lungs, but her own daughter, an incessant smoker, succumbed to a blood blockage in her lungs.

Seán MacBride used Ireland's neutrality during World War II to win concessions from the British for the Irish. A smart, hardheaded man, he rose to become chief of staff of the IRA, then minister of external affairs in the republic. He became active in human rights causes and a founding member of Amnesty International in 1961, along with the British human rights lawyer Peter Benenson. All the years MacBride spent jailed by the Irish Free State, the years he spent as a human rights lawyer defending his old IRA buddies, made him the right person to help form and then lead Amnesty International. Amnesty's stated mission is to help prisoners of conscience all over the world. In 1974, Seán MacBride won the Nobel Peace Prize for his international work. In his Oslo acceptance speech he said: "If those vested with authority and power practice injustice, resort to torture and killing, is it not inevitable that those who are victims will react with similar methods?" His mother who had expressed the same sentiment in different words, would have been very proud of her famous son. The irony of his having been IRA Chief of Staff, then awarded the most prestigious peace prize in the world, is notable.

Rather like his mother, Seán MacBride crafted his own image carefully, and would rearrange facts to make himself seem like an even more committed republican than he was, and at an even earlier age. His autobiography features few mentions of family. Although he attended university, he was on the run so much he didn't graduate. He impressively went to law school without an undergraduate degree. Like his mother, he was smart. The record he left the public was discreet. In his memoir he sidesteps family scandals: Iseult's illegitimacy; the charges his mother brought against his father; Maud's half-sister Eileen's marriage to his uncle Joseph MacBride, and the slew of cousins that resulted, many living in Mayo.

Maud's legacy in Ireland is an honored one for her children, grandchildren, and great-grandchildren. Through their many diverse activities throughout Ireland, her descendants remain part of her potent living legacy. Perhaps this book will help her be admired outside of Ireland too, as much as she deserves to be.

Epilogue

Last summer, miserable in 108-degree heat in Paris, reading Maud's denunciation of Dreyfus written decades after he'd been cleared of all charges and reinstated as a captain in the French Army, I asked myself if I really wanted to complete this project. I had uncovered complicated shadows to this woman's life—her deep-rooted, irrational anti-Semitism, her constant fabrications and embellishments, her absentee motherhood of her own children. It has been hard to like her.

But the complexity of Maud's character is one of the things that makes her a compelling figure, and her tireless efforts on behalf of human rights and Irish independence deserve respect. Against all odds, she made her voice heard in England, Europe, and the United States. So much of what she fought for and against, and so much of what caused her anxiety, are issues women are still grappling with today. So, despite those aspects of her life and beliefs that were difficult to accept, it seemed important to set the record straight.

Previous biographers have either accepted Maud's self-defined role as the Irish Joan of Arc, or alternatively focused on her life as Yeats's muse. In this brief book, I have labored to show her in the round, as a complex human being. She deserves to be admired for what she accomplished: pushing the door open so that other women could join the Irish nationalist movement. Of lasting significance is her lifetime of work on behalf of political prisoners, work that her son built on in creating Amnesty International, which continues to fight for human rights around the world.

Maud is interesting because of her complexity. She was a debutante and a rebel, a wealthy English Victorian woman who carefully crafted an Irish identity for the press and for the world. She betrayed her class by siding with the underdog, the vulnerable poor and the disenfranchised. In 1913 Jim Larkin led workers in a huge strike for a living wage in what became Dublin's greatest industrial struggle. The authorities and the Church were on the side of the magnates, another dreadful episode in modern Irish history. The workers lost, but Maud helped feed their children in Dublin during their strike, selling the last of her jewels to do so.

I empathized with her difficulties with men stemming from her elegant, appealing looks, her independent fortune, and her adoration of family members who died while she was young: first her mother, then her father. She had the characteristic sadness of a girl who lost her mother in early childhood. That seemed to have been the source of her huge empathy for unfortunates. Usually, she was on the side of the underdog, the most vulnerable members of society, including children, and I admired her empathy with those outside her narrow social circle.

Although a talented theatrical beauty, she questioned her own right to personal happiness. She had to be continually occupied, tied up with meaningful work for a grand cause. The poignancy of a young woman skeptical of the praise elicited by her own face and figures remains timeless. It was one I could relate to because after thirteen years at an all-girls school, having no brothers, and then tragically losing my older sibling—who until her illness was my role model—I found it hard to take my admirers seriously in college. I had never been on a "date" with a boy until then, and the clash between their attraction to my person and the terrible sense of desolation I felt within was too acute for me to process when I myself was just out of my teens.

Likewise, the question of how a woman with more money deals with a potential mate who has less remains relevant. Women continue to make political and economic strides towards equality in the twenty-first century but our success is by no means assured. All along the way, it has taken groundbreaking women such as Maud to lead us forward.

The role of obsession in art is fascinating and complex. The role of obsession in love is equally interesting. My professional obsession with Maud Gonne has ended with the completion of this book. Yeats wondered whether it was only his yearning after Maud that drove him toward a mastery of words with which to win her and express his frustrations. Obsession can drive the creative work of an artist and open individuals up to what Proust called the malady of love.

Yeats and Maud's enduring caring relationship can serve as an example of obsessive love. Strange though it may appear to those hearing their story for the first time, and although it sometimes tests credulity and defies conventional resolution, I believe very strongly that their relationship should be celebrated. Those who yearn helplessly to possess another human being, body and soul, express an elemental part of human experience, one that we can observe rather than judge.

Even as she aged, Yeats returned to Maud again and again in his magical poems. I found inspiration in Maud's great passions and life's work, seeing how raising her voice in public and on the page had a considerable effect in England, France, and the United States. She's become something of a role model for me. Maud's advocacy for human rights, the rights of political prisoners to be treated like human beings, rather than animals, resonates in our turbulent time, when dictators have popped up all over the world, across a wide variety of geographies and cultures. No one who reads about Maud's life can argue that one woman's voice can't make a difference in the world. She was much more than a muse.

It seems fitting that just as I finished this epilogue I met my cousin, newly moved to New York City, at the statue of Joan of Arc on Riverside Drive at 93rd Street. I had never known it was there in my neighborhood. The statue, I learned, was erected in 1915, during Maud's lifetime, and I reflected on how the fabulously inventive

Maud took on the mantle of Joan of Arc, six centuries after the young Joan was burned at the stake. Maud made Joan relevant half a millennium later to contemporary women, including the two great-granddaughters that I met. I am grateful to Maud Gonne for the journey she has taken me on, writing a contemporary biography of this multifaceted woman, building on the work other writers and scholars have done before. My quest to discover the source of my strange empathy with and fascination for Maud Gonne has ended.

May 8, 2020
New York City

Acknowledgements

I am grateful to Betsy Davidson for urging me to complete the project when I considered quitting, and to Betsy Sussler and Jennifer Danner for their encouragement, to Victoria Rowan for her careful reading, and to my editor, John Oakes for seeing the project through to publication.

The following librarians gave me invaluable help: Mathieu Lescuyer at the Bibliothèque Nationale de France, Roslyn Waddy at the Library of Congress, Courtney Chartier among other standouts at the Stuart A. Rose Library Manuscript Archives and Rare Book Collection at Emory University, which contains Maud Gonne MacBride's letters and childhood photographs.

Kieran Owen did legwork for me in Ireland verifying quotes in multiple places in the National Library of Ireland. Adam Nossiter read through an early draft of the chapter, "Two Lovers Against Dreyfus."

Eli Diner helped with the endnotes.

There are too many more librarians to thank who patiently helped me sift through digital newspapers and magazines. They are my unsung heroes. Last, thanks to Laragh Stuart, Iseult White for sharing their time and their thoughts about their great-grandmother, Maud Gonne.

Selected Bibliography

Augusta, Lady Gregory. *Lady Gregory's Diaries, 1892-1902*. Edited by James Pethica. Gerrards Cross, Buckinghamshire: Colin Smythe, 1996.

Barnes, David S. *The Making of a Social Disease: Tuberculosis in Nineteenth-Century France*. Berkeley: University of California Press, 1995.

Bartlett, Thomas. *Ireland: A History*. Cambridge: Cambridge University Press, 2010.

Birnbaum, Pierre. *Anti-Semitism in France: A Political History from Leon Blum to the Present*. Oxford: Blackwell, 1992.

Cardozo, Nancy. *Maud Gonne: Lucky Eyes and a High Heart* New York: New Amsterdam Books, 1990, originally published 1978.

Cobban, Alfred. *A History of Modern France, Vol. 3: France of the Republics, 1871–1962*. London: Penguin Book, 1965.

Dormandy, Thomas. *The White Death: A History of Tuberculosis*. New York: New York University Press, 1999.

Ellman, Richard. *Yeats: The Man and His Masks*. New York: W. W. Norton, 1979.

Feldberg, Georgina D. *Disease and Class: Tuberculosis and the Shaping of Modern North American Society*. New Brunswick: Rutgers University Press, 1995.

Flannery, Mary Catherine. *Yeats and Magic: The Earlier Works*. Gerrards Cross, Buckinghamshire: Colin Smythe, 1977.

Foster, R. F. *W. B. Yeats: A Life, Vol. 1: The Apprentice Mage, 1865–1914*. Oxford: Oxford University Press, 1997.

Frazier, Adrian *The Adulterous Muse: Maud Gonne, Lucien Millevoye, and W. B. Yeats*. Dublin: Lilliput Press, 2016.

Furet, Francois. *Revolutionary France, 1770–1880*. Translated by Antonia Nevill. Oxford: Blackwell Publishers Ltd. 1992.

Gonne, Iseult. *Letters to W. B. Yeats and Ezra Pound from Iseult Gonne: A Girl That Knew All Dante Once*. Edited by A. Norman Jeffares, Anna MacBride White, and Christina Bridgwater. New York: Palgrave Macmillan, 2004.

Gonne, Maud. *The Autobiography of Maud Gonne: A Servant of the Queen.* Edited by A. Norman Jeffares and Anna MacBride White. Gerrards Cross, Buckinghamshire: Colin Smythe, 1994.

Gonne, Maud. *Maud Gonne's Irish Nationalist Writings, 1895–1946.* Edited by Karen Steele. Dublin: Irish Academic Press, 2004.

Gonne, Maud. Papers. Stuart A. Rose Manuscript, Archives, and Rare Book Library, Emory University.

Harper, George Mills. *Yeats' Golden Dawn.* London: Macmillan, 1974.

Hone, Joseph. *W. B. Yeats, 1865–1939.* Middlesex, England: Penguin, 1971.

Jackson, Alvin. *Ireland, 1798-1998: War, Peace and Beyond.* Chichester, West Sussex: Wiley-Blackwell, 1999.

Jeffares, A. Norman. *W. B. Yeats: Man and Poet.* New York: St. Martin's, 1996.

Lee, Joseph. *Ireland, 1912–1985: Politics and Society.* Cambridge: Cambridge University Press, 1989.

Lee, Joseph. *The Modernisation of Irish Society, 1848–1918.* Dublin: Gil and Macmillan, 1973.

Londraville, Janis and Richard, eds. *Too Long a Sacrifice: The Letters of Maud Gonne and John Quinn.* Selinsgrove: Susquehanna University Press, 1999.

Lyons, F. S. L. *Ireland Since the Famine.* London: Weidenfeld and Nicolson, 1972.

MacBride, Seán. *That Day's Struggle: A Memoir, 1904-1951.* Edited by Caitriona Lawlor. Blackrock: Currach Press, 2005.

McAuliffe, Mary. *Dawn of the Belle Époque: The Paris of Monet, Zola, Bernhardt, Eiffel, Debussy, Clemenceau, and Their Friends.* Lanham: Rowman & Littlefield Publishers, 2014.

McAuliffe, Mary, *Twilight of the Belle Époque: The Paris of Picasso, Stravinsky, Proust, Renault, Marie Curie, Gertrude Stein, and Their Friends through the Great War.* Lanham, Maryland: Rowman & Littlefield Publishers, 2014.

McCoole, Sinead. *Easter Widows.* London: Doubleday Ireland, 2014.

McMillen, Christian W. *Discovering Tuberculosis: A Global History, 1900 to the Present.* New Haven: Yale University Press, 2015.

Nash, Linda. *Inescapable Ecologies: A History of Environment, Disease, and Knowledge.* Berkeley: University of California Press, 2006.

Rothman, Sheila. *Living in The Shadow of Death: Tuberculosis and the Social Experience of Illness in American History.* New York: Basic Books, 1994.

Toomey, Deidre, ed. *Yeats and Women.* New York: St. Martin's, 1997

Ward, Margaret. *Maud Gonne: Ireland's Joan of Arc.* London: Pandora, 1990.

Washington, Peter. *Madame Blavatsky's Baboon: A History of the Mystics, Mediums, and Misfits Who Brought Spiritualism to America.* New York: Schocken, 1995.

White, Anna MacBride and A. Norman Jeffares, eds. *The Gonne-Yeats Letters, 1893–1938.* New York: W.W. Norton, 1992.

Yeats, W. B. *The Collected Poems of W. B. Yeats.* Edited by Richard J. Finneran. New York: Macmillan, 1991.

Yeats, W. B. *The Collected Works of W. B. Yeats, Vol. III.* Edited by William H. O'Donnell and Douglas N. Archibald. New York: Scribner, 1999.

Yeats, W. B. *Essays and Introductions.* New York: Macmillan, 1961.

Yeats, W. B. *Memoirs of W. B. Yeats: Autobiography and First Draft Journal.* Edited by Denis Donoghue. London: Macmillan, 1972.

Notes

Prologue

"This war is inconceivable": Maud Gonne to W. B. Yeats, August 26, 1914, in *The Gonne-Yeats Letters, 1893–1938*, ed. Anna MacBride White, A. Norman Jeffares (New York: W.W. Norton, 1992), 347.

The last American biography: Nancy Cardozo, *Maude Gonne: Lucky Eyes and a High Heart* (New York: New Amsterdam Books, 1990, originally published 1978).

"as a child creativity was my friend": "The Mindfulness Workout by Iseult White," Writing.ie, April 12, 2018, https://www.writing.ie/interviews/the-mindfulness-workout-by-iseult-white/.

The very title of a 2016 biography: Adrian Frazier, *The Adulterous Muse: Maud Gonne, Lucien Millevoye and W. B. Yeats* (Dublin: Lilliput Press, 2016).

Chapter 1

"The concern became one of the largest": *Dictionary of National Biography*, 2nd Supplement, Vol. 1(1912), s.v. "Sir Francis Cook," by Charlie Welch.

Edith brought a dowry: Frazier, *Adulterous Muse*, 15.

That's $27 million today: For all conversions of historical pounds into current dollars, I have relied on the methodology and converter developed by Eric W. Nye. "Pounds Sterling to Dollars: Historical Conversion of Currency," University of Wyoming, https://www.uwyo.edu/numimage/currency.htm/.

William Gonne left Ireland: Gonne to W. B. Yeats, November/December 1905, *Gonne-Yeats Letters*, 220.

An estimated quarter of the island's population: Alvin Jackson, *Ireland, 1798–1998: War, Peace and Beyond* (Chichester, West Sussex: Wiley-Blackwell, 1999), 69.

"a mechanism for reducing": Quoted in Mic Moroney, "Descent from Grace," *Irish Arts Review* 29, no. 4 (2012), 125.

"The judgement of God": Quoted in Mary Daly, "Revisionism and Irish History: The Great Famine," in *The Making of Modern Irish History: Revisionism and the Revisionist Controversy*, ed. D. George Boyce and Alan O'Day (London: Routledge, 1996), 84.

"the Irish were a backward people": F. S .L. Lyons, *Ireland Since the Famine* (London: Weidenfeld and Nicolson, 1972): 176.

Changed her from a frivolous girl: Gonne to M. J. McManus, 22 January 1950, M. J. McManus Papers, box 1, folder 15, Burns Library, Boston College.

In 2016 it was the world's number one cause of death: World Health Organization, *Global Tuberculosis Report 2019* (Geneva: WHO, 2019), https://apps.who.int/iris/bitstream/handle/10665/329368/9789241565714-eng.pdf?ua=1.

An estimated one in four deaths: "Timeline," TB Alert, accessed April 30, 2020, https://www.tbalert.org/about-tb/tb-in-time/tb-timeline.

"I had gone to find Mama": *The Autobiography of Maud Gonne: A Servant of the Queen*, ed. A. Norman Jeffares and Anna MacBride White (Chicago: University of Chicago Press, 1995), 11. Gonne originally published her *Autobiography* at age seventy-two, in 1938. The queen of the title is Mother Ireland, not Queen Victoria.

"a sociable soul": *Autobiography*, 17–18.

A doctor recommended a more appealing climate: *Autobiography*, 25.

"No place has ever seemed as lovely": *Autobiography*, 17–19.

"A kindly stupid woman": *Autobiography*, 19.

"Hooray, Hooray, hooray!": *Autobiography*, 23.

"I do so wish I was with you": Thomas Gonne to Maud Gonne, December 21 [No Year], Maude Gonne Papers, box 1, folder 16, Stuart A. Rose Manuscript, Archives, and Rare Book Library, Emory University (hereafter cited as Gonne Papers).

"I am every day expecting a charming letter": Thomas Gonne to Maud Gonne, Gonne Papers, July 12, box 3, folder 6.

Maud recalled in her memoir as being "gloomy": *Autobiography*, 14.

"You must never be afraid of anything": *Autobiography*, 11.

"At first I ran all the time": *Autobiography*, 14.

"She succeeded in making us love our lessons": *Autobiography*, 25.

"It is such a pleasure to know": Thomas to Maud, Gonne Papers, box 3, folder 7.

"You must not run any risk": Thomas to Maud, Gonne Papers, box 3, folder 1.

"Having a great desire to be grown up": *Autobiography*, 27.

"people would take us for a honeymoon couple": *Autobiography*, 27.

"after one that suits you." *Autobiography*, p.34.

Maud paid attention and used a perfume as an adult that was recognized by
Yeats. Deirdre Toomey, *Labyrinths: Yeats and Maud Gonne.* Yeats Annual
no. 9, p. 122, note 8.

"an exquisite little flat": *Autobiography*, 33.

Sometimes she and the secretary quarreled: *Autobiography*, 34.

"women must be beautiful": *Autobiography*, 33.

"at a fashionable hotel": *Autobiography*, 34.

Tommy swooped in and took Maud away: *Autobiography*, 35.

Chapter 2

"It was the eviction I saw in 1885": Interview with Maud Gonne, January
22, 1950, M. J. McManus Papers, box 1, folder 15 Burns Library, Boston
College.

"They would stop us hunting": *Autobiography*, 41–42.

Maud laughed at him: *Autobiography*, 49.

Demonstrations in Trafalgar Square: Maud Gonne, "My Reminiscences," *An
Phoblacht*, March 1, 1930.

The plot of *Heartsease* was based on the Alexandre Dumas play *La Dame Aux
Camelias,* which came out the year before in 1848.

"sanitarium, a word used to describe many spas": T. M. Daniel, "Hermann
Brehmer and the Origins of Tuberculosis Sanatoria," *International
Journal of Tuberculosis and Lung Disease* 15 no. 2 (February 2011): 161–162.

"Sufferers seek hope": Gregg Mitman, "Geographies of Hope: Mining the
Frontiers of Health in Denver and Beyond, 1870–1965," *Osiris* 19 (2004):
93–111.

Today one spa treatment is named in honor of Eugénie. Other than managing
weight gain or loss, it is impossible to prove the health benefits of going
to a spa. I for one, having been to the spa at Royat, which I admired from

the outside, remain an admiring skeptic of their delicious sounding "health-improving" treatments. But I confess, I didn't try any of them, perhaps because they were so costly.

La Belle Meuniere: More than a hundred years later, La Belle Meuniere remains open. It serves fine Michelin-rated cuisine and has a lovely ambiance as well as a few rooms for romantic diners to spend the night upstairs after their meal, all housed under a Chinese red roof.

"Some diplomacy had to be exercised": *Autobiography*, 66.

"I kept wondering where I had met him before. At last I asked him. "But no, mademoiselle, it is impossible; I would never have forgotten if I had met you.": *Autobiography*, 62–63.

"Now we speak the same language": *Autobiography*, 65.3.

Chapter 3

"None of these ports are safe for a woman alone": *Autobiography*, 71.

"I, without a passport, carried to Russia": *Autobiography*, 82.

"life without a cause to work for would be very dull": Gonne to Yeats, 1911, *Gonne-Yeats Letters*, 256.

"There is nothing like work when one is unhappy": Gonne to Yeats, January 1900, *Gonne-Yeats Letters*, 119.

"preventing children of poor people": Jonathan Swift, "A Modest Proposal" (1729), http://www.gutenberg.org/ebooks/1080.

An idea that influenced the young Yeats: See David A. Ross, *Critical Companion to William Butler Yeats: A Literary Reference to His Life and Work* (New York: Facts on File, 2009), 512.

He advised her to read: Cardozo, *Lucky Eyes*, 66.

"She is no disciple of mine": *Memoirs of W. B. Yeats: Autobiography and First Draft Journal*, ed. Denis Donoghue (London: Macmillan, 1972), 43.

"I saw the most dazzling woman": Dominic Daly, *The Young Douglas Hyde* (Dublin: Irish University Press, 1974), 91.

For more on the uses of the words "republic" in France, see https://www.rosalux.eu/en/article/1498.french-republicanism.html for "the history of a mot voyageur, "a word that travels."

"Many took the habit of dropping in": *Autobiography*, 98.

"Being young and hasty": Maud Gonne, "Yeats and Ireland," in *Scattering Branches: Tributes to the Memory of W. B. Yeats*, ed. Stephen Gwynn (New York Macmillan: 1940), 19.

"The creatures, God help them": Maude Gonne McBride, witness statement, undated, WS 317, Bureau of Military History collection, Irish Defense Forces Military Archive, http://www.militaryarchives.ie/collections/online-collections/bureau-of-military-history-1913-1921/reels/bmh/BMH.WS0317.pdf.

"They are saying you are a 'woman of the Sidhe,' who rode into Donegal on a white horse surrounded by birds to bring victory." Autobiography, 134.

Millevoye only wanted Maud to work for Ireland: *Autobiography*, 139–40.

Describing the desolation she had seen in Donegal: *Autobiography*, 120.

She earned her first Dublin police report: Margaret Ward, *Ireland's Joan of Arc* (London: Pandora Press, 1990), 20.

Her picture was posted in the British society pages: Cardozo, *Lucky Eyes*, 79.

Susan too had trouble dealing with the harsh realities of life: R .F. Foster, *W. B. Yeats: A Life, Volume I: The Apprentice Mage, 1865-1914* (Oxford: Oxford University Press, 1997), 11, 21.

John Yeats never paid his debts: Foster, *The Apprentice Mage*, 7.

Yeats and his siblings lived most of the time with their grandparents: Foster, *The Apprentice Mage*, 19.

Willie had tea with plain bread and butter: Foster, *The Apprentice Mage*, 27.

Susan Pollexfen Yeats had suffered two strokes: Foster, *The Apprentice Mage*, 61.

"We were always paupers": Elizabeth Corbet "Lolly" Yeats's diary. Cited in Foster, *The Apprentice Mage*, 14.

"She is immensely tall": Quoted in Cardozo, *Lucky Eyes*, 3.

"I was twenty-three years old": *Memoirs of W. B. Yeats*, 40.

"Did I tell you how much I admire": Quoted in Ross, *Critical Companion*, 469.

"What wife could she make": *Memoirs of W. B. Yeats*, 42-43.

"White Birds": *The Collected Poems of W. B. Yeats*, ed. Richard J. Finneran (New York: Macmillan, 1991), 29.

"I was so proud of this exhibition": *Autobiography*, 209.

"She had come to have need of me": *Memoirs of W. B. Yeats*, 49.

"Cycles Ago": Foster, *The Apprentice Mage*, 116.

"When You are Old": *Collected Poems of W. B. Yeats*, 28; Foster, *Apprentice Mage*, 119.

Chapter 4

Within nine months, she returned to public life: Frazier, *Adulterous Muse*, 136.

"Un Peuple Opprimé": *La Nouvelle revue internationale* 8, May 15, 1891, 409-413.

She is pictured wearing pearls: *Le Voleur illustré, cabinet de lecteur universal*, February 11, 1892.

Clemenceau laughed and clapped himself on his thighs: Maurice Barrès, *Leur Figures* (Paris: Félix Juven, 1902), 245-248.

The man he bought those documents from had lied: Frazier, *Adulterous Muse*, 112–114.

Chapter 5

"I never willingly discouraged": *Autobiography*, 178.

"Who next?": Sean McConville, *Irish Political Prisoners 1848-1922: Theatres of War* (New York: Routledge, 2005), 367.

"More and more I realized": *Autobiography*, 304.

"It was exactly like the cage": *Autobiography*, 127.

"The movement of sympathy": *United Irishman*, July 2, 1892. The ardent and inventive Yeats had been the source for the claim of "2,000 articles," which he gave by letter to a writer friend who in turn included it in the *United Ireland* article. See: *Collected Letters of W. B. Yeats, Vol. 1, 1865–1895*, ed. John Kelly and Eric Domville (Oxford: Clarendon Press, 1986), 295.

NB: There is no way to verify the number of published newspaper and magazine articles on Maud in that particular year, though the Bibliothèque Nationale de France has amassed a collection of many thousands of French newspapers and magazines, and continues to add more. Meanwhile, its digital holdings for the French press for the year 1892 amount to only 1,280 publications. Of those, 69 results are produced when the name Maud Gonne is searched, an outstanding number that lends credibility to Yeats's claim of 2,000 articles appearing about Maud that year alone.

"her voice trembled and her eyes filled with tears": *Le Gaulois*, May 17, 1893.

"Following revelations by Miss Maud Gonne": *Le Figaro*, June 3, 1893.

Maud had these lucky tokens made into a brooch: Cardozo, *Lucky Eyes*, 147.

"Miss Gonne is a woman of heart": *La Revue Mondaine Illustré*, December 25, 1892.

When she had pneumonia: *Le Gaulois*, February 9, 1893.

"Maud Gonne is thin": *La Femme*, March 15, 1892.

"few people would be criminals": Maud Gonne, "My Experiences in Prison" (1919), in *Maud Gonne's Irish Nationalist Writings, 1895-1946*, ed. Karen Steele (Dublin: Irish Academic Press, 2004), 12.

"empowers any policeman": "Prison Bars" (1937) in *Maud Gonne's Irish Nationalist Writings*, 31.

"Prisons should be sanitary": "My Experiences in Prison," *Maud Gonne's Irish Nationalist Writings*, 15.

"It is hard to understand the mentality of gaolers": "Arbor Hill, Saoirse na hÉireann/Irish Freedom," (September 1936), *Maud Gonne's Irish Nationalist Writings*, 29.

Chapter 6

"The liberation of the traitor": Maud Gonne, "Foreign Correspondent," *United Irishman*, October 21, 1899.

"clenched fists and eyes full of menace": Raphaël Viau, *Vingt ans d'antisémitisme, 1889–1909* (Paris: Fasquelle, 1910), Chapter 8.

"In the old days when you were a Dreyfusard": Gonne to Yeats, October 4, 1927, in *Gonne-Yeats Letters*, 437.

May "like myself, was rather repelled": Gonne to Yeats, September 1900, *Gonne-Yeats Letters*, 134.

"proximity of Jew bankers": Gonne to Yeats, 27 July 1909, *Gonne-Yeats Letters*, 275.

"aimed at fir cones": *Autobiography*, 148.

Chapter 7

"I remember an embarrassed conversation": *Memoirs of W. B. Yeats*, 88.

"He Gives His Beloved Certain Rhymes": *Collected Poems of W. B. Yeats*, 63.

She had an occult vision: Gonne to Yeats, November 1895, *Gonne-Yeats Letters*, 54.

"She burst into tears" (1899): *Memoirs of W. B. Yeats*, 89.

"I saw much of Maud Gonne": *Memoirs of W. B. Yeats*, 104.

"We had fed the heart on fantasy": "The Stare's Nest by My Window" (1928), *Collected Poems of W. B. Yeats*, 211.

"For the honor of our country": Gonne to Yeats, November 14, 1895, *Gonne-Yeats Letters*, 55.

"The language is so lovely": Gonne to Yeats, April/May 1897, *Gonne-Yeats Letters*, 70.

"the perception of the spirit" Quoted in editor's note, *Gonne-Yeats Letters*, 63.

"It was a time of great personal strain": *Memoirs of W. B. Yeats*, 125.

"in a low voice that seemed to go through": *Memoirs of W. B. Yeats*, 112.

"Our friendship must indeed be strong": Gonne to Yeats, 1897, *Gonne-Yeats Letters*, 72.

"My letters are formal perhaps": Gonne to Yeats, September 6, 1897, *Gonne-Yeats Letters*, 76.

"I thought we were sufficiently friends": Gonne to Yeats, May 23, 1896, *Gonne-Yeats Letters*, 60.

"I heard much scandal": *Memoirs of W. B. Yeats*, 63.

"A shock to me": *Lady Gregory's Diaries, 1892-1902*, ed. James Pethica (Gerrards Cross, UK: Colin Smythe, 1996), 197.

"Words" (1910): *Collected Poems of W. B. Yeats*, 93.

"vile abandoned woman": *Gonne-Yeats Letters*, 93.

Yeats wrote a letter attacking Teeling: See Gonne to Yeats, March 1897, *Gonne-Yeats Letters*, 65.

"I see her standing with W. B. Yeats": Ella Young, *Flowering Dusk: Things Remembered Accurately* (New York: Longman's, Green, 1945), 54.

She makes the decision sound political: *Autobiography*, 100.

Maud made the first move: See Deirdre Toomey, "Labyrinths: Yeats and Maud Gonne," in *Yeats and Women*, ed. Deirdre Toomey (London: Macmillian, 1992), 96.

" a somewhat threatening erotic figure": Toomey, "Labyrinths," 98.

"touch her as one might a sister": *Memoirs of W. B. Yeats*, 133.

"I can do more": *Memoirs of W. B. Yeats*, 134.

Chapter 8

"I don't know whether things are well": Yeats to Lady Gregory, February 4, 1899, *The Letters of W. B. Yeats*, ed. Allan Wade (New York: Macmillan, 1955), 311–312.

"During the last months": Yeats to Lady Gregory, February 19, 1899, *Letters of W. B. Yeats*, 312.

She added a leather easy chair: Foster, *Apprentice Mage*, 187.

She insisted Yeats dissuade Maud: *Lady Gregory's Diaries*, 167.

She told him that Dr. Mark Ryan: Frazier, *Adulterous Muse*, 192.

"Whether you kill your enemies": *Autobiography*, 283.

"The tricks we used to play": *Autobiography*, 99.

"Suddenly, in a clear thrilling note": *Autobiography*, 229.

"a horror and terror of physical love": *Memoirs of W. B. Yeats*, 134.

"the end of the British Empire": *The Irish World*, February 10, 1900.

"What she says about the Boers": *The Boston Herald*, January 6, 1900.

"a new Joan of Arc": *The Blackfoot News*, January 20, 1900.

On her US tour, she raised $3,000: Editor's note, *Gonne-Yeats Letters*, 479. Inflation calculated based on the Bureau of Labor Statistics' Consumer Price Index, see inflation calculator at https://www.officialdata.org.

"For Victoria in the decrepitude": Maude Gonne, *The United Irishman*, April 7, 1900.

Griffith was outraged by Collis's assertion: *Gonne-Yeats Letters*, 122–3.

"I bought a new hat for the occasion": *Autobiography*, 201.

"What part of Ireland was he from": Frazier, *Adulterous Muse*, 198.

John O'Leary who sat next to Maud: Frazier, *Adulterous Muse*, 195.

Grown men and women would recognize Maud: *Autobiography*, 270.

"In a field . . . and in the presence": *The Collected Works of W. B. Yeats, Vol. III: Autobiographies*, ed. William H. O'Donnell and Douglas N. Archibald (New York: Scribner, 1999), 277.

After their break-up they remained sufficiently amicable: *Le Gaulois*, November 25, 1900.

Chapter 9

"Adam's Curse: *Collected Poems of W. B. Yeats*, 80.

"I saw the meaning of that strong beautiful chin": Quoted in Cardozo, *Lucky Eyes*, 170.

"I was doing a good act for my country": John MacBride Notebook, 1905, Fred Allen Papers, National Library of Ireland.

"Little sister, neither you nor anyone": Maude to Kathleen Gonne, Gonne Papers, box 1, folder 3.

"I lost my mother when I was very young": "Interview with Rebecca Tilney at City Gala 2018," Bionic Buzz, March 11, 2018, YouTube video, 1:02, https://www.youtube.com/watch?v=jFckwZUGzEs.

"We are made that way": Maud to Kathleen Gonne, 1902, Gonne Papers, box 1, folder 2.

"justified her Howth reputation as a healer": *Autobiography*, 305.

"I think I will be happy with John": Maud to Kathleen Gonne 1902, Gonne Papers, box 1, folder 3.

"MacBride is a man I know very well": Maud to Kathleen Gonne, 1902, Gonne Papers, box 1, folder 2.

Did not think Maud would make him happy: *Autobiography*, 349.

"She is accustomed to money:" *Autobiography*, 349.

Her daughter sobbed when Maud told her: *Autobiography*, 348.

"I felt like crying too": *Autobiography*, 348.

"Queen, forgive me": *Autobiography*, 348.

"a danger to the nationalist movement": Gonne to Yeats, September 9, 1903, *Gonne-Yeats Letters*, 172.

"Lambkin, don't do it": *Autobiography*, 348.

As the Irish nationalist movement became more extreme: R. F. Foster, *Modern Ireland, 1600-1972* (London: Penguin, 1989), 455.

"I want to look at truth": Maude to Kathleen Gonne, Gonne Papers, box 1, folder 2.

Les Mouettes was one of the sites selected for the famous landings for the D-Day Invasion of Normandy. In preparation, the Allies tore down the house.

"I'm afraid even the Church": *Autobiography,* 339.

She told her to marry in the English consulate: Foster, *Apprentice Mage,* 286.

"I will keep my own name": Gonne to Yeats, February 1903, *Gonne-Yeats Letters,* 167.

"Maud Gonne is about to pass away": Yeats to Gonne, January 1903, *Gonne-Yeats Letters,* 165.

"started on our honeymoon": *Autobiography,* 350.

"MacBride went to meet his friends": Editor's note, *Gonne-Yeats Letters,* 168.

That is what she wrote in a letter to Yeats: Gonne to Yeats, September 9, 1903, Gonne-Yeats letters, 175. She describes Eileen as "the little girl you may remember once having seen with my old nurse & who is now living with me as governess to Iseult."

"was protected by a group of young hurlers": Editor's note, *Gonne-Yeats Letters,* 172.

"with me the National ideal": Gonne to Yeats, September 25, 1903, *Gonne-Yeats Letters,* 178.

"From all I can hear": Gonne to Yeats, September 1903, *Gonne-Yeats Letters,* 174.

She condemned the play: Maud Gonne, *The United Irishman,* 24 October 1903.

"The King of Ireland has been born": Quoted in Ward, *Ireland's Joan of Arc,* 85.

Eileen Wilson, who had become acquainted with MacBride's brother: Gonne to Yeats, November 1905, *Gonne-Yeats Letters,* 216.

"who lives in Westport is quite sober": Gonne to Yeats, March 1905, *Gonne-Yeats Letters,* 197.

"she is downright ugly": John MacBride's observations on the evidence petitioner's witnesses, 1905, Frederick J. Allan Papers, National Library of Ireland.

He saw women as having to operate by different rules: Caoimhe Nic Dháibhéid, "'This Is a Case in Which Irish National Considerations Must Be Taken into Account': The Breakdown of the MacBride-Gonne Marriage, 1904-8," *Irish Historical Studies* 37, no. 146 (November 2010): 241–264.

"fresh from a Paris divorce court": "Why Marriages Fail," *Rockford Morning Star,* August 16, 1905.

"If John keeps from drink": Reproduction of letter from Maud to R. B. O'Brien, December 31, 1904, in John MacBride Notebook, Fred Allen Papers, National Library of Ireland.

"I hate to trouble you": Gonne to Yeats, November 1905, *Gonne-Yeats Letters*, 213.

"I'm glad you know all": Gonne to Yeats, January 1905, *Gonne-Yeats Letters*, 186.

Chapter 10

"I feel somehow that the Maud Gonne I have known": Quoted in Foster, *Apprentice Mage*, 293.

It has become fodder: The rumor is discussed in Foster, *Apprentice Mage*, 286; and stated as fact by Margaret Ward in *Ireland's Joan of Arc*, 87.

"I'm working at painting": Gonne to Yeats, July 15, 1905, *Gonne-Yeats Letters*, 178.

The relationship foundered: Roy Foster March, "Yeats: Love, Magic and Politics," *The Irish Independent,* March 2, 1997.

The Abbey Theatre Yeats founded in 1904 together with Lady Gregory, funded by his patron Annie Horniman, became an important institution on the international theater scene.

"It was hard leaving you": Gonne to Yeats, December 1908, *Gonne-Yeats Letters*, 258.

"His Memories": *Collected Poems of W. B. Yeats*, 223–224.

"We've so remade the world": *Memoirs of W. B. Yeats*, 173.

"Michael Angelo denied the power of sex": Gonne to Yeats, January 13, 1909, *Gonne-Yeats Letters*, 203.

"It really seems as if half of Paris": Gonne to Yeats, February/March 1910, *Gonne-Yeats Letters*, 287.

"Few Irish people can have fully realised": Maude Gonne, "The Children Must Be Fed," *Bean na hEirann*, May 1910.

"the hungry school children": Maude Gonne to John Quinn, February 19, 1911, John Quinn Memorial Collection, box 27, Manuscript and Archives Division, New York Public Library.

"to keep up the strength of the race": Gonne to Quinn, Quinn Collection, box 27.

"I like the poem so much": Gonne to Yeats, October 29, 1910, *Gonne-Yeats Letters*, 294.

"This war is an inconceivable madness": Gonne to Yeats, August 26, 1914, *Gonne-Yeats Letter*, 347.

"patching up poor mangled wounded creatures": Gonne to Quinn, January 7, 1915, Quinn Collection, box 27.

"I would like to go & stir": Gonne to Yeats, December 1914, *Gonne-Yeats Letters*, 352.

"within sound of the cannon": Gonne to Yeats, October 1, 1915, *Gonne-Yeats Letters*, 359.

"You I believe, still see beauty in war": Gonne to Quinn, July 30, 1917, in *Too Long a Sacrifice: The Letters of Maud Gonne and John Quinn*, ed. Janis and Richard Londraville, (Selinsgrove: Susquehanna University Press, 1999), 206.

John MacBride was among the executed: Shane Hegarty and Fintan O'Toole, "Easter Rising 1916—the aftermath: arrests and executions," *Irish Times*, March 24, 2016.

"Easter, 1916," *Collected Poems of W. B. Yeats*, 180.

"a fine one... the best end possible": Quinn to Gonne, July 29, 1916, *Too Long a Sacrifice*, 172.

"The rector made a very eloquent speech": Quoted in Caoimhe Nic Dhaíbhéid, *Seán MacBride: A Republican Life, 1904–1946* (Liverpool: Liverpool University Press, 2014), 18.

Chapter 11

"jam Sean's very allergic head": Iseult Gonne to W. B. Yeats, May 25, 1918, *Letters to W. B. Yeats and Ezra Pound from Iseult Gonne: A Girl That Knew All Dante Once*, ed. A. Norma Jeffares, Anna MacBride White and Christina Bridgewater (Basingstoke: Palgrave Macmillan, 2004), 102–103.

"active medical and open-air treatment": Quoted in Dhaíbhéid, *Seán MacBride: A Republican Life*, 26.

Maud had become reluctant to join: Margaret Ward, *Ireland's Joan of Arc*, 120.

The death of the great man troubled her: Maud Gonne MacBride to Ethel Mannin, February 10, 1948, National Library of Ireland.

The Irish army's intelligence unit opened a file on her: W.J. McMormack, *Blood Kindred: W.B. Yeats, The Life, The Death, The Politics* (London: Pimlico Random House, 2005), 106.

"Let no more young lives be sacrificed": Maude Gonne, "The Request," *Irish Times*, May 10, 1946.

she wrote letters as part of a campaign: See Nancy Cardozo, *Lucky Eyes*, 407 for details and quotes from Maud Gonne's letters to Ethel Manin from the National Library of Ireland.

"My father wasn't, she was": Quoted in Emily Hourican, "Carving a Life Out of Destruction," *The Irish Independent*, May 31, 2009.

But her daughter was not so lucky: *Dictionary of National Biography Online*, see s.v. "Stuart [née Gonne], Iseult Lucille Germaine," by Deirdre Toomey, accessed April 1, 2020, https://doi.org/10.1093/ref:odnb/72587.

"If those vested with authority and power practice injustice, resort to torture and killing, is it not inevitable that those who are victims will react with similar methods?": Seán MacBride, "The Imperatives of Survival," in *Les Prix Nobel en 1974* (Stockholm, 1975), 209.

Index

About the Author

Kim Bendheim is a poet, performer, and writer. Her byline has appeared in *The Forward, The Nation, The Chicago Tribune, Ladies Home Journal, The New York Times, The Los Angeles Times,* and *Bomb magazine,* which published her poetry. A cum laude graduate of Harvard University, she received two Masters degrees: one from New York University (where she studied Irish literature and history), and one from the City College of New York (where she studied poetry). She lives in New York City.

Printed in the USA
CPSIA information can be obtained
at www.ICGtesting.com
JSHW022345251223
54314JS00006B/32